Aug 13, 2019

Joy, you are a woman
of valor!

Rejoicing in Him,

Dick & Mary

Matt 5:10

Mighty Man of Valor

One Man Against the Odds

BY

Stephen John Goundry

Bloomington, IN   authorHOUSE   Milton Keynes, UK

AuthorHouse™
1663 Liberty Drive, Suite 200
Bloomington, IN 47403
www.authorhouse.com
Phone: 1-800-839-8640

AuthorHouse™ UK Ltd.
500 Avebury Boulevard
Central Milton Keynes, MK9 2BE
www.authorhouse.co.uk
Phone: 08001974150

First published by AuthorHouse 3/3/2006

ISBN: 1-4208-5809-2 (sc)

Library of Congress Control Number: 2005905244

Printed in the United States of America
Bloomington, Indiana

This book is printed on acid-free paper.

To my wonderful sons

David and Jonathan,

God's own mighty men of valor

TABLE OF CONTENTS

FOREWORD

Why are so many ministers leaving their pastorates after only a few years in leadership? Why are so many men quitting the ministry altogether, forsaking their calling for secular employment? Clearly, there is a fundamental problem that needs addressing. Present day statistics in these matters have become a trumpet call, blasting out a warning to all those who desire to spend their lives serving God. Dealing with the realities of Christian service, this book, Mighty Man of Valor endeavors to encourage men to "face the truth," "endure the hardships," and "finish the race!"

It is the author's prayer that all who will read and digest this book will be strengthened in their sense of personal destiny and that in these times, God will elevate them to lead the way and cause them to be "pillars" in the house of God.

May the Lord increase our ranks with --------

"The mighty man, and the man of war, the judge, and the prophet, and the prudent, and the ancient; The captain of fifty, and the honorable man, and the counselor, and the cunning artificer, and the eloquent orator."

ISAIAH 3 v 2, 3

INTRODUCTION

The plain truths about Christian ministry, with all its joys and hardships, are rarely, openly discussed. Yet periodically the wreckage of ministers' lives float by us in the statistics of modern-day Christian service. It shocks us that so many ministers leave their pastorates after only two or three years of service—many of them never to return to any form of ministry. Many leave with one main thought in their hearts—"I didn't know that ministry was going to be like this!" This book will help you to understand the realities of Christian ministry, and will provide the tools and preparation you will need to become a mighty man of valor, one who overcomes the enemy's attack and builds the kingdom of God.

It has become obvious that many men assuming the position and responsibilities of Christian leadership have not been adequately prepared. The realities have been hidden from the eyes of a great majority of people who enter the ministry—a fact evidenced by the rise of "burn-out," the failure of many to resist the temptations of leadership, and the domestic tensions in the homes of many ministers. Because these ministers have not been armored with the truth, somewhere along the line they have bought into a dream of what ministry should be, only to have their expectations shattered. Somebody has not told them sufficiently what the costs of serving God can be.

When Saul of Tarsus, later, the apostle Paul, was converted through a dramatic encounter with the Lord Jesus, one of the first things the Lord did for him was to give him the truth about his life and ministry. The Lord showed him plainly that he was going to be used in a mighty way, but added to the menu of his life was a great deal of personal suffering for Christ's Name. No fluff, no dreamlike images of empty notion, he was told plainly what to expect. From the inception of his ministry, this beloved apostle built his life upon the realities of God's Word. With grace he embraced the heavenly concoction of "sorrowful, yet always rejoicing" (2 Corinthians 6:10). This is the cup that the Lord gives to all His ministers to drink — and that's the truth!

Truth is not that readily accessible in the world in which we live. Most of the time this world turns on the *razzle-dazzle* of the upbeat comments of the confident. The masses long to hear only what they want to hear, and the loud, swelling words coming from ambitious leaders inevitably produce a hopeful *make believe* world of wealth, health, and happiness. Continual upbeat talk certainly has its value, for where would any of us be in a life without a positive outlook, but talk without substance becomes the salesman's charming pixie dust to obscure the view in order to clinch the deal. The glitter of the moment will eventually disappear, revealing the lack of real foundation.

Reality, that enemy of empty rhetoric, will always show its unwanted face at some point along the way. Sometime, somewhere, someone is going to stand up like the little boy in the classic story and tell the world that which the world secretly knows—namely, "the Emperor has no clothes!" To the embarrassment of everyone, the outspoken truth will turn every face red, and although appreciation for discovery will be given at first, the world will not hold dear the *whistle blowers* who put their necks on the line. Initial thanks and acclaims for courage will give way to an eerie silence as prospective employers fear that the *torch of truth* might shine into the dark corners of *their* business!

Truth is light, and light brings exposure. How we need it; how we hate it! Although we spend a lot of time ignoring it or even suppressing it, the truth of a situation usually breaks out and the *overhang* of lies and half-truths crumble in the dust. Then the masses wake up out of their willing intoxication, shake themselves vigorously, and begin to make sober investments of their time and money.

In recent years, a dear friend of mine took hold of the reins of an investment company known for its conservative approach. As of today, He has had the joy of more than quadrupling the company turnover. His company did not promise dizzy high interest gains like others, or employ salesmen who with tempting words, offered their clients risky products with dubious projections. While the *"razzle-dazzle"* upbeat party music of the market place was being cranked out, his company caught the attention of only a small percentage of investors, but when the *music* faltered, the fortunes of his company began to increase dramatically as edifices of "make-believe" crumbled and the lack of substance was exposed. When my friend was asked how he had accomplished so much success, he replied, "It's because there is a market for truth!" He further amplified his words by stating the public's distrust in the wake of huge losses and that they were now inclined to invest their money more wisely.

The "market for truth" has emerged again in our present times, and is having an effect on all of us in many ways. As the power icons fall and uncertainty faces us all, we have begun to hunger for reality. We are refusing the "sirens" lure because we are regularly confronted with the wreckage of other ships reported strangely missing in the night. We are clamoring for the truth. We want to know—it's as simple as that!

In ministry as in business, the realities of ministry require nothing less than *men of valor* who are willing to *"grasp the nettle"* whether public or private. We must meet the challenges with courage, fortitude, and stamina. These are the basic requirements to work for God in a world that not only resists His Spirit, but also will at times openly engage in warfare against Him. If Christ Himself is the greatest Person that ever came into this world, and if His work on Calvary was the greatest accomplishment this world has ever known, then it follows that His continued ministry through the saints is the greatest activity that is going on in this and every age.

Is it any wonder that those who perform this service should find themselves in the war of the ages? To all who will be soldiers for the cross of Christ, there is given a battle tunic for service, a weapon to make war and the assured prospect of ultimate victory with all its spoils. Having said that, it must also be said that no one is given immunity from the slings and arrows of life's conflicts. However, we are promised this one thing—the Presence of the Lord, even unto the end of the age. His awesome Presence, and His personal involvement in our work will take an ordinary man like Gideon and transform him into a mighty warrior. It is accomplished through these precious words:

The LORD is with you, you mighty man of valor!

—Judges 6:12

CHAPTER ONE
THE EYES OF HEAVEN

The story of Gideon only begins when the charm of *"doing what was right in their own eyes"* had been thoroughly broken. The seductive thoughts of unbridled personal liberty along with unrestricted behavior had cast its spell on Israel, but the Lord was leading them on a path of repentance. It was a path that would lead the nation back to God.

The national stupor had been rudely awakened again by the cruel realities of war. When truth has *"fallen in the streets,"* it's only a matter of time before God, the Judge of all, restores the moral balances of a nation. When a nation sends true judgment into reverse gear, makes justice a stranger, and bars the way for equity, a cry from the righteous goes up to heaven. The eyes of heaven look down upon the people with mercy, searching for a man to stand in the gap to intercede for the land. The Lord is always looking for a man who has not compromised his

1

integrity in this world and He will listen to the prayers of a righteous man and answer his requests in powerful ways. If, for whatever reason, intercession is not made, then the Lord will clothe Himself for war, and the Spirit of the Lord will lift up a standard against the enemy and He will redeem the situation by Himself! (Isaiah 59:16-19). It is sad but true to say, that when men are left to their own devices, they always seem to stray away from God rather than draw near to Him. Thankfully, God's mercy is greater than our disobedience and so the Lord rescues His people from the enemy and more often than not, delivers them through the most unlikely of individuals! Gideon was such a man.

The Party's Over

For the children of Israel, *"playtime"* in the nation was now truly over. The bell had rung, and people were running for cover. The windy rhetoric of marketplace prophets had fallen silent as the overhang of borrowed time was finally breaking up. The enemy was back at the gates again, and fear gripped every heart. The events now transpiring had not come totally unexpected, for a pattern of oppression had emerged in preceding years, that when Israel had sown their crops, the enemy would pour into the land like a great flood. The men of Israel seemed to have no power against them, for the enemy came into the land as far as Gaza and annually, the produce of the nation was either siphoned off or taken with violence. Everyone in Israel now acknowledged the sobering reality of the nations' situation. They could no longer kid themselves that everything was all right. The bubble had burst, and pretence, rather than truth, had become the first casualty of war. There now existed a market for truth!

JUDGES 6:1-6

1.Then the children of Israel did evil in the sight of the Lord. So the Lord delivered them into the hand of Midian for seven years, 2. and the hand of Midian prevailed against Israel. Because of the Midianites, the children of Israel made for themselves the dens, the caves, and the strongholds which are in the mountains. 3. So it was, whenever Israel had sown, Midianites would come up; also Amalekites and the people of the East would come up against them. 4. Then they would encamp against them and destroy the produce of the earth as far as Gaza, and leave no sustenance for Israel, neither sheep nor ox nor donkey. 5. For they would come up with their livestock and their tents, coming in as numerous as locusts; both they and their camels were without number; and they would enter the land to destroy it. 6. So Israel was greatly impoverished because of the Midianites, and the children of Israel cried out to the Lord.

The eyes of the Lord had filled with sorrow as the children of Israel had repeatedly sinned in His sight. He had seen it all. He'd seen the secret things, and He had seen the open things. It was time for Him to act.

The Day of Midian

For seven years God had allowed the Midianites and other eastern tribes to consume the land of Israel and to prevail over it. They destroyed everything they could and left little in their wake except carnage. Fear of these enemy raids had caused the children of Israel to flee to the mountains for protection, where they made dens and places of refuge in the caves.

Sadly, this situation was not a new one. In times past the nation had gone through multiple cycles of defeat and deliverance in their relationship with God. Whenever Israel had departed from the Lord and had broken His covenant, they always suffered at the hands of their enemies until the Lord raised up a "Deliverer" to break off the yoke of oppression. As long as the "Deliverer" lived, the people followed the Lord, but after his death, the people strayed away once more, proving the fact that godly leadership is vital to the well being of a nation. Time and time again, history proves that "righteousness exalts a nation, but sin is a reproach to any people" (Prov. 14:34). When corruption at the highest level becomes the main course of the day, is it any wonder that the people become sick? One must never underestimate the influence of the *man of God*, for the Scriptures have recorded that when the man of God is not present, the "golden calf " always seems to arrive—brought in by people who should know better! (See Exodus 32:7–10).

At the time of our story of Gideon, there was a certain irony in the fact that it was Midian who was oppressing the children of Israel. The Midianites were the posterity of Midian, a son of Abraham! This son of Abraham, born to his wife Keturah, had produced descendants who inherited a dominant streak as they, through their generations, enjoyed prominence among the children of the East. The clan of Midian had gained the upper hand over the dreaded Amalekites, and even over all the Ishmaelites, in the time of Gideon.

The Midianites had blessed Israel by preserving the life of Jethro the priest, who was also Moses' father-in-law. But they had been nothing but trouble to the children of Israel since that time, and eventually they degenerated to the same low level of animosity that Ishmael and his descendants had for the seed of Isaac. The Midianites had shown their belligerence to Israel by their wiles, tormenting them and tempting them to sin. By doing this, they succeeded in causing the Israelites to weaken the covenant they had with God.

One of the last things God commanded Moses to do before his death was related to the punishment of Midian. Although Moses had indeed brought punishment to the people of Midian, by the time of Gideon, the remnant of evil Midianites had once again vaunted themselves into a place of prominence. Now the armies of Midian marched confidently at the head of a confederation of nations bent on the destruction of Israel. The opportunity to humble Israel and take the spoils through plunder became impossible to resist, and so they made their customary plans for war, not realizing that this time, God Himself had ordered the battle!

The Midianites didn't see what the eyes of heaven were seeing. They were blinded to what was really going on. The God who can make even "the wrath of man" to praise Him was about to accomplish His purpose on both Israel and Midian (See Psalm 76:10). For Israel, seven years of oppression was about to end. For Midian, slaughter had been determined. God was going to strike the Midianites with such a blow that the whole event would eventually become a proverb in Israel. Future mass slaughters of the enemy would be referred to obliquely by, *"as in the day of Midian."* (See Isaiah 9:4) The Midianites and the children of the East had brought their sins to the boiling point. Little did they know that the *sword of the Lord* was unsheathed against them! Although they came in droves, their *overhang* of arrogant pride was about to collapse, and they couldn't read the signs. They adorned both themselves and their camels with gold, and they covered the land like a swarm of grasshoppers. It looked as if it was going to be easy, just like before. But they were up against a covenant-keeping God. There would be deliverance for the Israelites; but for the Midianites there would be destruction.

Reading the signs

Throughout history, it has often been seen retrospectively that before disaster struck, warning signs of imminent catastrophe were there to be read. The question often asked afterwards is *"Why were the warning signs ignored?"* What is it about some people that makes them impervious to *the winds of change?* Empires that have willingly ignored the fresh breezes of an approaching new era have been eventually caught up in a whirlwind of violence. The good times of dominance and power with all its abundance are eventually forgotten. Believing that their rule was going to last forever and intoxicated with their national pride, they failed to see the cauldron around them that was brewing a revolutionary drink called *Independence.* When warning signs of unrest have been continually ignored, the day of reckoning finally arrives and conciliatory words fall on deaf ears. Nothing but *unconditional surrender* will satisfy and the demands of the moment will not rest until a new flag is flying in the sky.

Every man of God must be able to read the signs around him. How can you be a servant of God if you can't perceive what the will of your heavenly Father is? How do you know *what* He wants done? How do you know *when* He wants it done? As a man, do not let the dominance of your natural eye blind you to invisible realities! Let us learn from men like Bartimaeus who despite being blind, could see that Jesus was more than just a Nazarene, and cried out to the Lord in Messianic language saying, "Jesus, Son of David, have mercy on me!" Bartimaeus not only saw Jesus of Nazareth as a prophet, he saw him as a king! (Mark 10:47). Success in God for everyone is largely due to understanding times and seasons and the best way to secure this awareness in your life is to have a higher opinion about God and a lower opinion about yourself! If you will walk carefully before the Lord and keep your heart pure, He will reveal His thoughts into your mind. If you continue to serve the Lord with loyalty, He will make you like Abraham, your first father in the Faith and elevate you to become a *"Friend of God"* (Isaiah 41:8). Jesus told his disciples that if they did everything he commanded them, they would not only be his servants, but they would be his friends.

They would be men who knew what their master was doing!

The Word of God tells us that in David's time, there were mighty men from the tribe of Issachar who joined their lives to David, because they had understanding of the times and they knew what Israel ought tó do (1 Chron 12:32). Let us learn from them.

Chapter Two
The Voice of the Prophet

As we look closer at the story of Gideon, we see that God set in motion a sequence of events that would bring ultimate restoration to His people. By looking at these events, we can get a better understanding of the ways of the Lord.

The children of Israel finally recognized that as a result of their own selfish living with no regard for the covenant they had with God, their enemies were now bearing down on them, and they were in a hopeless situation. With nowhere to turn, once again they cried out to the Lord:

So Israel was greatly impoverished because of the Midianites, and the children of Israel cried out to the Lord.

—Judges 6:6

It does seem that when your life is under threat, and when you have little to eat, it is very easy to receive the *"spirit of prayer and supplication!"* The Lord, in His wisdom, has many times chosen to heat up the battle to bring a nation to a crisis point before He steps in to remedy the situation. When a nation is in the "crucible," a cry to heaven always seems appropriate, even in the most secular of societies. When Great Britain was in its darkest hours during World War II, the highest authorities in the land called for days of prayer and fasting. Such public requests to God in times of safety and of plenty would have been met with derision. But it has been noted throughout history that in times of national emergency, a heartfelt cry to the living God is rarely ridiculed. After the disastrous events of September 11th 2001, prayer times in the United States were treated with great respect. There was very little scornful laughter for religious sentiment at that time, because prayers were comforting the nation in a time of great loss. Special days were set aside to remember those who were grieving and local churches were filled to capacity in the ensuing days. Many in the nation prayed prayers of remembrance and those who understood, prayed prayers of repentance. Desperate times call for desperate measures! In times when no one else can help, a cry will always go up to heaven.

JUDGES 6:7-10

7. And it came to pass, when the children of Israel cried out to the Lord because of the Midianites, 8. that the Lord sent a prophet to the children of Israel, who said to them, "Thus says the Lord God of Israel: 'I brought you up

from Egypt and brought you out of the house of bondage;
9. 'and I delivered you out of the hand of the Egyptians
and out of the hand of all who oppressed you, and drove
them out before you and gave you their land. 10. 'Also I
said to you, "I am the Lord your God; do not fear the gods
of the Amorites, in whose land you dwell." But you have
not obeyed My voice.'"

The *"spirit of prayer"* is a manifestation of God's Holy Spirit, Who is dispatched by the Lord to place the burden of the Lord into the hearts of His people. For a short time, as God's people receive the concern of God into their hearts, this burden becomes the joint property of the people of God. They carry this burden *"in the spirit,"* and through intercessory prayer they start to lift the *weight* of that burden back to God, who *first* gave it! Arriving on the wings of prayer, the burden of the Lord is heard in heaven. It will be only a matter of time before the Lord responds with His Word.

The release of God's Word is the start and finish of everything. Once spoken out of heaven, God's Word never returns back to God without accomplishment.

So shall My word be that goes forth from My mouth;
It shall not return to Me void,
But it shall accomplish what I please,
And it shall prosper in the thing for which I sent it.

—Isaiah 55:11

Many things may still have to take place on earth before God's perfect plan of redemption is completed, but as far as heaven is concerned, His Word has already gone forth! It's basically all over. A decision from God is final! How awesome is this – yet how comforting. Every man of God should know the power of a " *Word from the Lord.*" No word from God falls to the ground empty. Every word from God produces exactly what it was sent to do! – and exactly on time!

In the story of Gideon, the people had cried unto the Lord, and now He was responding. Out of obscurity, an unnamed prophet receives the response of God. He is given a message and a voice with which to proclaim the message. Prophets are messengers sent from God to release the mind of God into a situation. By so doing, the eternal aspect of God's Word is released into time. He, who is beyond the bounds of time, sends a man to speak in time to affect both time and eternity. How awesome is this ministry of speaking the Words of God! It carries power in all realms, because the "golden thread" of the Word conveys the essence of an infinite God!

Simply put, if the Lord has not spoken, then nothing will happen! God is always looking for faithful men who will speak His Word here on Earth, and that is why a minister of Christ must be an able minister of His Word. The minister's work is to deliver God's messages through sermons. The ministry of Christ can take many forms, but the primary form of communicating God is through the preaching and teaching of God's Word, both that which is written in the Scriptures and that which is heard directly in the heart. Not withstanding, any Word from God into the heart will never contradict the

Word already revealed in Scripture, for *what is written is written,* and there is an objective finality about the Holy Scriptures.

This ministry of speaking God's Word is prophetic by nature, because the Holy Spirit, who is the *"Spirit of prophecy,"* inspires it. The Holy Spirit comes to reveal, through words, what has already been decreed in heaven. When He comes upon a person in prophetic unction, it's difficult for that one not to prophesy! (Jeremiah 20:9). God was now using this unnamed prophet to speak to the nation in its hour of crisis, and they were ready to listen. As in this case, when God uses a man's voice to release that word of power on Earth, things change. Its power begins to work immediately. Atmospheres change, incidents occur that alter people's long-held views, and attitudes improve with hearts becoming more responsive to the things of God. It might not be so obvious at first, but, to the discerning eye, there are signs of a radical change emanating from the spiritual world.

This ministry gift is of great importance to any community of believers. It is of immeasurable worth to those working on the mission fields, in that it reveals the mind of God in their situation. The reward of receiving a prophet is that the revelation he brings will establish the work in wisdom, knowledge, and understanding. There are times when the Lord will *not* speak, and He will test you in areas of trust, in order that your relationship as a son can be further developed, but most of the time He wants you to understand what His mind is in the circumstances of your life.

Relating to God in this way is the kind of relationship that Jesus talked about with his disciples. From the earliest times in His ministry, Jesus taught his disciples to pray, saying, "Our Father in heaven" (Matthew 6:9) and after his resurrection, he told them that he was ascending to not only His Father, but their's too! (John 20:17). Every believer is a son and the happiest sons are the ones who obey God and take His advice. In addition to such a friendship with God, the prophetic word will keep you on the right course. If we are left to our own devices, there are times when we can so easily choose the wrong path. The apostle Paul had this experience when he was preparing to go to Asia and Bithynia (Acts 16:6–8). The Holy Spirit gave him revelation, forbidding him to enter into those parts, having another strategy for the work in His mind.

In our story of Gideon in Judges 6, the prophet declared to the children of Israel what the mind of the Lord was concerning them, and as is so often the case with prophets, he spoke directly and plainly to them. Through the prophet's words, the Lord reminded them of their history. He said, *"I brought you up from Egypt and brought you out of the house of bondage...and out of the hand of all who oppressed you, and drove them out before you and gave you their land"* (Judges. 6:8–9). Then came the stinging indictment from heaven with these piercing words: *"But you have not obeyed My voice!"* (v. 10)

It appears quite clear that in walking with God through this life, everything seems to hinge on obedience to His voice. In a former land of other gods and in a surrounding world of enemies, shouldn't the children of Israel have been more attentive? Sadly one fact is true in any generation—the hardening of the heart always seems to produce a deaf ear, not only to God, but also to men. How difficult it is sometimes to get a man just to listen! "Arrogance is tied to the tongue of the proud," and proud men would rather hear *themselves* speak than listen to somebody else.

Walking with God requires ears that can hear the still, small voice of God over the clamor of an ungodly world. Just as God revealed Himself to Elijah through a still, small voice, He will often speak in quietness today (1 Kings 19:12). A "gentle and quiet spirit" (1 Peter 3:4) does not belong solely to the heart of a good woman, for any man of valor needs to know when it's time to talk and when it's time to be silent. There is a time to stand up, and there is a time to keep your seat! Can you be sensitively submissive to discern the moment? Only the obedient man can make true success a lifetime partner, for it is the obedient man who continually finds himself in the right place at the right time! Is it any surprise that such a man as this will always find himself joined to the prophetic? Even if he is not a prophet, his life will always be compelling, and his words will always minister "life." But oh...watch out when you are around an obedient prophet, because his voice carries weight! To such a man as that, God has given him the "voice of Judah" (Deut. 33:7). Even if he speaks softly, that man of God will always bring the "shout of a king" into your life! (Numbers. 23:21).

The Prophet's Experience

While it is true to say that every man of God should have the *touch of the prophetic* in his life, it remains a fact that it is the Lord who sets prophets in the kingdom. No man can make himself a prophet. To those who are called to be prophets, the ministry can start to take place virtually at any time in life, but it is usually done at a time when a minister has developed maturity through experience. The demands of this ministry require the very best a man can offer.

The prophetic office requires a man to handle the Word of the Lord without damaging it, and then to faithfully deliver it to the people. Many men have answered the call of God to stand in the office of a prophet, both in Old and New Testament times. One of the first lessons the apprentice prophet must learn is the difference between a *calling* and a *sending*. This is sometimes a little difficult, because the anointing of the prophet begins to rest upon him long before he is sent by God and invested with the full powers of his office. The Lord allows the prophetic mantle to rest upon him so that he can learn the moving of the Spirit and be trained in the administration of the prophetic. Elisha received his master's mantle over him long before Elijah was taken from him so that he could learn the ways of the prophetic. It was also a sign to him that one day the prophetic anointing upon Elijah would rest upon him.

This moving of the Holy Spirit upon a young man is not restricted to the prophetic ministry, for even Samson experienced the sacred activity of the Spirit of God when he was preparing for ministry in the camp of Dan. It is recorded that young David was anointed with the Spirit of God long before he became king, and he learned the ways of God through years of experience as he prepared for his accession to the throne of Israel. The Holy Spirit's presence rests upon all those preparing for ministry, but there are some common denominators of experience among those who are in God's school of the prophets.

1.   They are all immobile in their life's work until God initiates the ministry.

2.   They all hear or see revelation of one degree or another.

3.   They are all compelled to speak because of the unction of the Holy Spirit, which is operative in them.

4.   They all possess the authority of God in their words and actions.

5.   They all seem to arise at crisis times or just before.

6.   They all receive resistance and persecution for their ministry.

Prophets are brought into closer communion with God than are regular preachers. The preachers deliver the message, but very often the prophet not only delivers the message—he IS the message! Sometimes the prophet is a sign in himself! This close identification with the mind of the Lord puts this kind of ministry on a much higher level. Such was the experience of John the Baptist, for when the people asked him who he was, he replied, "I am the voice of one crying in the wilderness: make straight the way of the LORD" (John 1:23).

The ministry of John was a sign from God that a new dispensation was about to unfold and that the Baptist himself was a confirmation of that fact. So it is today, that when the Body of Christ sees the advent of certain kinds of prophetic ministries, they are to be seen as heralds of what the Lord is doing in the world. As time marches on toward the consummation of the age, God will send many prophets to the Body of Christ with an exciting yet most sobering of ministries, and they will all share a common theme. Their message will be, "Behold, the Bridegroom is coming; go out to meet him!" (Matthew 25:6).

The prophet Ezekiel became as one with his prophecies when he ate the scroll of God's words. In a spiritual vision, the prophet had to digest the words of God that were being revealed to him. The contents were sweet to receive but difficult to administer, because the words of God were heavy with judgment. Ezekiel received an arduous task, but he was compelled to speak out! Sometimes, the opposite experience happened to him, and nothing came out of his mouth because God wasn't saying anything to the people. Then the prophet became a sign of God's silence.

This identification with the "fellowship of His suffering" cost these men very dearly. They suffered hardships as a prophetic sign of forthcoming judgments. For example,

18

one day God told the prophet Ezekiel that he was going to suddenly lose his wife, and that he wasn't allowed to weep over her passing! This was to be a prophetic sign that God was suddenly going to take away His beloved temple from among the people. On another occasion, the prophet Hosea took an unfaithful woman to be his wife, to show a prophetic picture of how Israel was treating the Lord, her husband! True ministry costs.

The Burden of the Prophet

The courageous prophet will bear the weight of God's concerns. God's gift to the prophet is His burden, and it is through the "burden of the word of the Lord" that the prophet will find the unction to prophesy. The burden of the Lord is the concern of God that sits like a weight upon the prophet's heart. While this is particularly the case in the ministry of a prophet, once again, these events are not restricted to prophets, for all men of God should know something of these spiritual manifestations in their lives.

I well remember having this experience myself when ministering in an ancient Russian city some years ago. Waking up at around four o'clock in the morning, my chest felt unusually tight. Knowing that it wasn't anything to do with my supper the night before, I asked the Lord what the burden meant. Immediately, in my inner mind, I saw a picture of the head of William Shakespeare and the words, "To be or not to be, that is the question!" I understood immediately that God was revealing to me somebody's problem with suicide. No sooner had I grasped the concept of what the Lord's concern was then another vivid picture quickly appeared before my mind. I saw a door, belonging to a building in that particular city. On the side posts of the door, there were markings in blood, which served as counters of all those who had passed through that door, and of those who would pass through in the future.

I understood clearly that one of the Lord's concerns for that particular city was the alarming rate of suicide that prevailed there. The deep despair of many centuries had cast its shadow over the present generation and if left unchecked, would claim more lives in the future, because those who went through the "door" did not return! That day I shared this message with the Bible College students I was teaching at that time. After they had verified the vision with local statistics, we prayed together for a long time about this issue, asking God to forgive the past and bless the future with real hope. We prayed for the life of God to be in the city, and for the love of God to manifest - which is the answer for all men, everywhere, and at all times.

Simply put, the "burden of the word of the Lord" is given so that we may understand by *spiritual weight* what the mind of God is on any subject. Therefore, we must keep an open mind to the things of the Spirit of God and a soft heart to receive the feelings of God.

Prophets Today?

A question often asked is, "Do we need prophets today?" While it is true to say that the prophets in the

Old Testament did have a unique standing with God, it can be clearly seen in many New Testament writings that the office of the prophet still has a role to play. The wonderful fact of the born-again experience, with all its glorious truths about believers being the sons of God, has still left room for the prophetic gifts in this life. As sons of God, we are led and guided by the Spirit of God. The Chief Shepherds' voice resides within us. But, from time to time, we still need to hear from God from outside ourselves.

There will indeed come a day when prophecy will be needed no longer, when even faith and hope will have finished their course, but until then, while we are still seeing the eternal through a dark glass, let us welcome the gift of the prophet amongst us. We need prophets. We need them to give confirmation, direction, and revelation to individuals, churches, and nations!

There are prophets in the Body of Christ today who are gifted and courageous to speak the mind of God into our lives. Here are some common denominators in the performance of their ministry, which are characteristic of them all.

1. They live out the very heart of God.
2. They show by the Spirit things to come.
3. Through the gifts of the Holy Spirit, they reveal things hidden in the past.
4. They reveal the hearts of people now.
5. They bring to the Church doctrinal truths that have been lost or forgotten.

6. They give the mind of God to individuals, churches, communities and nations.

Known by God

In the story of Gideon, the prophet that God used was unnamed. This is a very important aspect of serving God because so many of God's works are accomplished by people who are content to serve without the praise of men. Many of God's heroes receive no rewards for service in this life, but heaven has recorded everything and when the *"books are opened,"* (Revelation 20:12) every man will be judged according to his works. This challenge comes to us all, because we secretly love the praise of men and the adoration of women. The incessant drive within us for respect can propel us into doing reckless things. The jails are full of young men who in a moment of pride, put themselves into needless jeopardy just so that they could vaunt their *street credibility* within their circle of friends. How many times have you heard men say, *"I just wanna be somebody!"* To become "somebody" in the Lord, a man must first become a "nobody" - and be happy about it! Will you allow the Lord to lead you into a small place? Will you allow Him to take you into a prison experience like innocent Joseph and prepare you in secret? Will you allow God to take you away into a private desert experience like John the Baptist and the apostle Paul before He sends you forward? Can God bypass you and make somebody else the temporary "center of attraction"? Can you wait for as long as it's necessary before the Lord is able to launch you into the limelight? Can you be content like Jesus to be a craftsman for years until God says "It's time!"

These are the invisible challenges that come to all men of God. These challenges must come because the "man of valor" must know the God of Heaven intimately. He must get to know his heavenly Father, the One who sees in secret (Matthew 6:18). After the secret battles with the giants of *fame* and *fortune* are won, the man of God walks free from the crippling need of the adulation of others. Like the unnamed prophet in this story of Gideon, he will be content just to be known by God. If you can win in secret, you can triumph in the broad light of day. Never underestimate the power of that personal victory and don't think you will never have to fight those worldly giants again!

CHAPTER THREE
I SOUGHT FOR A MAN AMONG THEM

<hr>

S ome of the most haunting words ever spoken are recorded in the Book of Genesis, when God came into the Garden of Eden and said, "Adam! Where are you?" Just as He was searching for our first father, so the Lord searches for willing hearts among the sons of Adam. Having committed the dominion of this world to Adam and his race, God will always look among the sons of Adam to find at least one man who will say, "Not my will, but Yours be done!"

I can almost hear the conversation between the celestial *watchers* as they ask themselves the question, "Is there a man among them that will pray with sincerity, 'Thy kingdom come, Thy will be done, on Earth as it is in Heaven?'"

JUDGES 6: 11-16

11. Now the Angel of the LORD came and sat under the terebinth tree which was in Ophrah, which belonged to Joash the Abiezrite, while his son Gideon threshed wheat in the winepress, in order to hide it from the Midianites. 12. And the Angel of the LORD appeared to him, and said to him, "The LORD is with you, you mighty man of valor!"

13. Gideon said to Him, "O my lord, if the LORD is with us, why then has all this happened to us? And where are all His miracles which our fathers told us about, saying, 'Did not the LORD bring us up from Egypt?' But now the LORD has forsaken us and delivered us into the hands of the Midianites."

14. Then the LORD turned to him and said, "Go in this might of yours, and you shall save Israel from the hand of the Midianites. Have I not sent you?" 15. So he said to Him, "O my LORD, how can I save Israel? Indeed, my clan is the weakest in Manasseh, and I am the least in my father's house." 16. And the LORD said to him, "Surely I will be with you, and you shall defeat the Midianites as one man."

As a direct result of God hearing the prayers of His people and the resultant prophetic word, the Lord now begins to act in tangible, visible ways. The man of the hour must be found! "Where is the man who will trust Me with his life? Where is the man who, with great private courage, will say *Yes* to My will and find that place of abandonment where he can say, "If I perish, I perish"? Is there a man who will go with Me into the *"dead zone"* and pass the point of no return to make himself a candidate for My supernatural power?"

Divine Encounter

Gideon must have thought to himself, *"Who is the stranger under the tree? Where did he come from, and how long has he been watching me?"* At this point in the story, Gideon was full of apprehension and in great fear about the current events. Any onlooker at that moment would have been forgiven for thinking that Gideon was *not* the man God was looking for.

But, whatever Gideon appeared to be or not to be, the question of whether he was God's man had already been settled in heaven. The "eyes" of Heaven see every thought and every motive within the human heart, and within this man, Gideon, the Lord had seen *His man!* Clearly, the man God chooses to engage the enemy in the public arena will have passed the private tests of life successfully. The first thirty years of Jesus' life on earth were spent largely in private settings, but the testing of those years in secret became the bedrock of His successful public ministry later.

As the apostle Paul wrote in one of his letters, God will always first test a man privately in the natural order of things. He does this in order to ensure the successful handling of the true spiritual things later, for if a man cannot handle the natural order, how will he be able to manage the spiritual order that comes later? As it was

27

with Gideon, so it will be for us. First the natural order, and then the spiritual.

Before the prophetic word came to Barnabas and Saul to release them into apostolic ministry, the Holy Spirit had already called them and prepared them for that work. As a safeguard for prophecies of a governmental nature, God will never immediately send someone into an apostolic ministry without calling and preparing them first.

Before Gideon could think about much, the Lord in angelic, yet manly form, spoke a word into Gideon's life that absolutely transformed him: "The LORD is with you, you mighty man of valor!" (v.12). What a wonderful example of the faith of God! On the surface of things, it seemed like a total contradiction of the facts. It looked as if the Lord was not with Gideon or his nation, and that Gideon was anything but a man of valor while hiding by the winepress! Ah! The power of God's Word! It can speak into any situation and bring light into the deepest darkness. It creates order where there is chaos and turns defeat into victory!

God's Word can create something from nothing and make a frightened man into a national hero. Gideon stepped forward and began to converse with this strange, but heartwarming messenger. He questioned the comment made about the Lord being with him. Confused by his present-day reality, Gideon asked the question of the moment: "If the Lord is with us, why is all this happening?" The calamity now facing the nation was puzzling, causing Gideon—and others—to simply conclude that the Lord must have left them.

And the Lord Looked Upon Him

There has always been something awesome about the face of the Lord. An encounter with the Divine is a beautiful, yet frightening prospect. Throughout history, it is only on rare occasions that men have been permitted to see some manifestation of the Godhead. How wonderful it must have been to see Jesus of Nazareth! To have walked with him and seen his tender, yet resolute eyes look at you (and through you) must have been inspiring and unnerving all at the same time. How dreadful Peter must have felt after failing the Lord so badly, when on the eve of the crucifixion, as he was denying Jesus, the Bible says, "the Lord turned, and looked on Peter."

Happy is the man who sees the gentle face of the Lord, but woe to that man who beholds the "wrath of the Lamb," for then no one is able to stand! From our first father's failure in the Garden of Eden, we have this fearsome warning about the countenance of the Lord, because God didn't ask Adam to leave the Garden—He drove him out!

This basic understanding of beholding both the goodness of God and the severity of God is fundamental to the continued success of the man in ministry. This combination of love and fear is the necessary balance to maintain a successful position with God over a whole lifetime. If a man of God is deficient in any of these aspects, he will suffer loss somewhere along the way. To omit the *fear of the Lord* is to underestimate the authority of His throne and how great a King He is. Men who have no fear of God don't understand how strict their Heavenly Father can be and they are totally shocked when discipline is administered to them. They secretly think that God would never remove them from their position or that He would ever put them in jail! But to omit the *love of God* is to completely misread the benevolent intentions of His heart. God loves all his sons and will interject His correction to keep them from falling into the condemnation already sentenced on the world.

Go In This Your Might!

So, the Lord looked kindly upon Gideon and said, "Go in this might of yours, and you shall save Israel from the hand of the Midianites" (v. 14). At this point, Gideon is still not fully realizing who this person is who is talking with him, yet somehow he automatically yields to the inherent authority of the stranger. Gideon's perspective begins to broaden as the stranger continued talking. "Have I not sent you?" He asks Gideon.

This whole conversation was now beginning to grip Gideon, and a new ray of perception was dawning in his heart. However, he began to do what many other timid, frightened souls have done throughout history—make excuses to God. A negative response is never pleasing to God, and excuses have never worked with the Lord. "Go!" He told Gideon, "Just go, mighty man of God!"

So many men are resisting the call to *go* because they are waiting for something spectacular to drop out of heaven into their lives. They are always waiting on heaven to propel them forward, when God has already asked us to overcome our own inertia and take a step in the right direction. There is no doubt that God does endue with power, but most of the time, men go out in the strength which they already have, however small. They go out trusting the One who has sent them. Waiting on God is good, but there comes a time to go, and that is the time when He *opens the door.*

You must go *then!* and resist the temptation to analyze everything first. The door of opportunity will not always be available! Doors open, and doors close. Heaven opens the door, but heaven can't wait forever. If you won't go, then somebody else will, and that person will be rewarded accordingly. There will always be the temptation to wait for the circumstances to be favorable, but God sometimes sends His man at the worst time possible.

Most prophets are sent at difficult times, because their ministry is to step into the current crisis and speak for God. This is what Joshua experienced. The Jordan River was overflowing its banks, but he went when God said, and the Lord worked a wonder for him as the children of Israel went over on dry ground! The supernatural had intervened again, but only after obedience, and only after the priests bearing the ark of God had committed themselves to the water. Only when their feet were wet did the supernatural take place, and that incident became a permanent lesson to all of God's people. In most circumstances, the supernatural takes over only after the natural has been exhausted!

A friend in England once told me a simple example of stepping out in faith to see God work the supernatural.

He said, "When an airplane begins to make a flight, it taxi's out onto the runway, and after clearance, it begins to build up speed for the takeoff. At forty miles an hour, the plane can quite easily stop. At seventy miles an hour, the plane can still stop with a bit of a screech from the wheels. But at one hundred miles an hour, the plane must go up! The runway is coming to an end, and as the plane reaches that point of commitment—another law greater than gravity comes into the equation. At that point, aerodynamics begin lifting the plane into the air!" So it is in matters of faith. When the man of God has reached the point of commitment of "no going back," when his feet are truly wet, then the Lord begins to lift the vision.

Brave Heart

True valor is found in the willingness to take true risk. Throughout history, events have taken place that demanded courage of the highest order. Faced with overwhelming force in the heat of battle, one man's bravery has produced a victory through unusual effort, and that victory has won the day. The impetus one man can give can never be underestimated. Sometimes the risk taken has ended in personal sacrifice, but has still won the day, because time was won and the position was held.

Every man wants to walk away from the battlefield and receive his commendation, but few are willing to go into an "Alamo" situation where there is no escape once engaged in the battle. To enter into the Alamo was to knowingly cross the point of no return. Such willingness divides the men from the boys.

The *flesh* wants to live. It wants the glory. But they that live *after the flesh* will find it impossible to please God in this life. The carnal man will always seek cheap glory and secretly make contingencies in light of possible failure. But the man of valor will follow the Lord anywhere, even into a situation where there are no back doors of escape.

This is the dividing line among the servants of God. There are those who are willing to lose nothing, and those who are willing to risk everything. The King Saul's of this world can only look over their shoulders in jealousy when the stone from the pure man's sling has just felled the giant. Men like Saul are reduced to the role of spectator when the David's of this world run past the point of no return to see the supernatural work on their behalf! When David confronted Goliath, that day the victory belonged to David, because God had given it to him in response to his willingness to "lay it all down."

A Christian businessman in Northern Ireland once told me a story about a conversation he had with a fellow businessman. The other businessman had made a lot of long-term investments. Almost overnight, one of his investments prospered. Someone asked this businessman if he felt a little guilty about making so much money so quickly. He replied with this comment, "If I put it down, I have the right to take it up again!"

The man who will lay it down and run the risk has the right to take up the reward, even if it is after only two or three days. David's bravery against Goliath that day became a pattern for others. Later, many of his mighty men would exemplify the same brave heart.

One of the most notable of David's mighty men was a man called Benaiah. The Bible says that he "had gone down and killed a lion in the midst of a pit on a snowy day" (2 Sam. 23:20). This incident had all the hallmarks of true valor, because not only was it risky to take on a lion in a pit, but added to that was the fact that Benaiah did it on a snowy day! It is very difficult to get in and out of a pit at the best of times, but when icy snow is lining the inner walls, a decision to fight a lion inside becomes even more daring. Benaiah must have known that in such circumstances it was either himself or the lion. There was only going to be one winner! True valor demands true risk, and the eyes of heaven discern the brave heart even when men cannot see the difference.

I Will Be With Thee

Gideon received the guarantee of heaven, which is ultimate victory. The path before him was littered with obstacles, but victory would be the final outcome. Let every man be emboldened with this thought: If God is with us, the mission *will* be successful as far as heaven is concerned. We must go. We must wage war and win the day! Through our obedience, the Lord will give authority to the "soles of our feet," and we will be able to take dominion over the enemy.

What matters to God is this: Does He have the right man for the job? Has His search among men found the willing vessel He needs to turn the situation around? May we never underestimate the dynamics of one man under God. One man with God's blessing upon him becomes the catalyst for changing events. The Lord will always challenge men to shoulder responsibility, because the blessing of God flows from the head and shoulders of the man of His choice. The authority of God always flows down, as did the anointing oil on Aaron the high priest of God. (Almost all the holy garments that Aaron wore were put on him from the top of his head and then down his body.)

Because most of us live in a democratic environment where all men are viewed equal, it is difficult to appreciate the dynamics of a monarchy. It is important to remember that the kingdom of God is not established from the *floor up*, but from the *throne down*! Theocratic government is the order of the day in heaven. When the call of God comes down to His children, it's not a case of "we the people." It's strictly a case of "You are the man!" You are the choice of God when He calls you into office and *not* the popular vote of men.

When you are knocking down the giants, "You are the man!" But be warned, because when you are trying to cover your private sins, it is still a case of "You are the man!" Such is the nature of serving the living God. The ministry of the Church is a holy thing. The Lord has sanctified it, and if any man would engage himself in it, he must know that the rewards are vast but the disciplines for pollution are heavy.

Nevertheless, be prepared, like Gideon, to commit your way unto the Lord and to trust that He who calls is He who keeps. Remember also, that if one man under God can achieve so much, what can a *nation* under God achieve for Him? Let every man who calls the United States of America his country, let him earnestly pray that his beloved nation would remain a nation *under God*! Blessed is the nation whose God is the LORD! (Psalm 33:12).

Chapter Four
Confirming the Call

===============

Gideon was like any other man that has been chosen by God to accomplish great things for the kingdom in that he needed confirmations of his call. The Lord was kind to him and gave him some wonderful experiences to strengthen his will and build his confidence for the task ahead. Supernatural signs were given because supernatural signs were asked for. Gideon wanted to know for sure that God was going to save Israel by his hand and so he asked the Lord to do something remarkable.

JUDGES 6:36-40

36. So Gideon said to God, " If You will save Israel by my hand as You have said – 37. look, I shall put a fleece of wool on the threshing floor; if there is dew on the fleece only, and it is dry on all the ground, then I shall know that You will save Israel by my hand, as You have said."

38. And it was so. When he rose early the next morning and squeezed the fleece together, he wrung the dew out of the fleece, a bowlful of water. 39. Then Gideon said to God, " Do not be angry with me, but let me speak just once more: Let me test, I pray, just once more with the fleece; let it now be dry only on the fleece, but on all the ground let there be dew." 40. And God did so that night. It was dry on the fleece only, but there was dew on all the ground.

If the secret of successful ministry is Gods' man doing God's work, then it follows that God's man must have God's assurance. God's calling rings clear within the pure heart of a man of valor. This inner sense of destiny can be resident even within the life of a child, as was the case with young Jeremiah who was called to a prophetic ministry while still in the womb of his mother! (Jer 1:5). Truly, divine ministry is discovered in time but originates in eternity. In fact, everything God does has an eternal perspective, for He is the 'Ancient of Days...whose goings forth are from of old, from everlasting' (Dan. 7:9; Mic. 5:2).

Man is a creature of time. From the dust he was taken, and to the dust he will return. God Almighty is not bound to our circle of life but is supercelestial as on one hand, He governs the whole universe and on the other hand, He sits on the circle of the earth. He rules everything. He is the Eternal Light that continues to extend itself without conclusion. He is linear in His approach, for His eternal light shoots forward, with neither curve nor "shadow of turning" (James 1:17).

Our God goes on and on, for He is without horizon and there are no limits upon His experience. As for us, well, we play our part in His ongoing purposes. This life of ours is His gift to us. It can be truly said that the man who has responded to God's call at the first hearing is the most blessed among all who walk on this earth. Invariably, the man who resists God's call in his life with words like, "No, Lord," or "Not yet, Lord," finds himself in many of life's sorrows and eventually full of regret at the missed opportunities.

Whenever God finds a man who will say, "Yes, Lord!" He will command the blessing of confirmation upon his life. God will strengthen that man and confirm his path with many signs and tokens of His will. He will establish His will by speaking directly to him as His "chosen vessel." The greater the "step of faith" that is required, the greater the confirmations that he will receive along the way. Gideon saw God confirm his call to service with two supernatural signs in two nights. The Lord wasn't angry with him for asking for one more sign because all of His purposes are established by at least two or three witnesses. When Joseph interpreted Pharaoh's dreams of seven years of plenty and seven years of famine, he knew that the dream was from God because it was " repeated to Pharaoh twice!" (Genesis 41:32). The admonition of the Scriptures tells us that "By the mouth of two or three witnesses every word shall be established" (1Cor 13:1).

Sadly, many men who have heard the call of God have not waited patiently for the second or third confirmations of the call and as a result, have ran straight into failure.

Ironically, you can be the right man with the right kind of ministry, but if it's not the right time, it still doesn't work! Heaven endorses only that which is on time. Gideon was proving to himself that he was God's man for the hour and that it was God's time for the job to get done. The second confirmation of a dry fleece upon a wet ground calmed his fears and sealed his will from that time forward. He now had all the principles of successful ministry in order. He was the right man with the right ministry at the right time!

In cases where there is misalignment of these principles, when ministers of God have not waited on the Lord for His full confirmation, the collateral damage can be heavy and it can take a long time for spouses, family and associates to heal from the whole experience. Many years ago, a minister of great standing in the Lord, being used mightily by the Holy Spirit, had a vision to go to Australia. The vision to go and minister in Australia had come as no surprise because he had secretly desired to visit that country for many years. Immediately, he put his house on the market and uprooted his family from their home and within the shortest of time spans, found himself, his wife and kids on an aircraft bound for Australia. This man was one of the most anointed men of God I had ever seen, having many signs and wonders in his ministry. He thought that when he got to the "Land down under" that his Holy Ghost ministry would just "take off." However, the opposite happened! Faced with bitter disappointment, he cried to the Lord one day and said, "Lord, what is happening? I obeyed the vision you gave?" A voice came back to him and said, "Did I tell you to go? Did I confirm the time of the vision?" The minister quietly repented for his presumption and asked his family and friends to forgive him for all the upheaval his decisions had brought them. He returned home and decided to wait on the Lord for His perfect timing. May you like Gideon, watch for the confirmation of God's timing so that the victory is guaranteed. Don't let the enemy trick you into doing something before its perfect time. Sometimes, when the enemy can't get the man of God to sin, he will try to get him to do something foolish and in haste. Many men of God have at some time heard a voice suggesting that they do something radical for God and for them to do it very quickly. But it has proved to be the voice of the "Tempter" who spoke a similar word to the Lord Jesus when he suggested that he should throw himself down from the pinnacle of the temple. Don't be like some missionaries who were working in the jungles of the Far East and were hindered in their arduous journey by a fast flowing river. Thinking to themselves that as the apostle Peter had walked on water, so *they* could also! Sadly, their bodies were found downstream some days later. The truth is that the apostle Peter walked on water only after the Lord had said, "Come" (Matt 14:29). Peter himself was looking for a word from the Lord to confirm his decision. Be sure that the voice you are hearing is really the voice of God. Don't be deceived into doing something that came as a suggestion from the tempter and not from God. During His forty-day wilderness experience, Jesus was taken by the devil to the pinnacle of the temple and the tempter said to him, "throw your self down" (Matt. 4:6). Thankfully, the Lord knew that it was not His Father giving Him that advice.

He recognized the voice of the tempter and neutralized that single voice. His discernment is an example to us of how to carefully discern the voice of the enemy and to wait patiently to hear God's confirmation to govern our lives.

Waiting on the Lord

The Bible tells us clearly, "To everything there is a season, a time for every purpose under heaven" (Eccles.3:1). Everything that God does is very good and it's exquisitely appropriate. "Everything is beautiful in its proper time." Heaven reflects His handiwork. It's not called Paradise for nothing! Even the Heavenly City itself shines with resplendent glory as its wonderfully aesthetic design refracts so much light. A thing of beauty is a thing worth waiting for! This is how the patriarch Jacob must have felt when he first cast his eyes upon Rachel. She was so beautiful to look upon, he decided that she was worth waiting for. For Jacob, this beautiful woman had enraptured his heart and held for him the prospect of heaven on earth. God knows how to make a "Rachel." He knows how to create a thing of beauty. He knows how to put the glorious finishing touches on anything He makes. This is what He did for Job when all of his trials were completed. He gave him three special daughters of whom it was recorded, "in all the land were found no women so beautiful as the daughters of Job."

The Garden of Eden was not just an amalgamation of good things; it was a creative collection of heavenly splendor from the brush strokes of the great Artist! The architectural glory of His throne and dominion were diffused into the softer lines of nature, allowing man to live and move within the more gentle order of God.

As it was in the Garden, so it remains today. We can understand the wonderful mind of God through His creative work. The unapproachable light that surrounds His throne has now shone through the prism of His Creation. The rays of light surrounding His glorious Presence bless the Earth with the refracted glow of His peace and goodwill to all men. As we allow the "Day Star" to arise in our hearts, we will begin to perceive the seasons that God has planned for our lives and we begin to have understanding of our times. As we follow His continuous direction, we begin to know the God "which was, and is, and is to come" (Rev. 4:8).

The dark clouds of our fallen world begin to break up in the light of God's face. As we discern the hidden things of God, we commence our path of true enlightenment. We see that Almighty God did not merely design the ages of time—He has already finished them! It's all over as far as He is concerned! He wins! And everyone who has been created in Christ Jesus shares His victory! Rewards will be given to all true men of valor, for every man who has overcome in this life has been promised a place at His throne.

Acceptance of the sovereignty of God is fundamental to the success of any ministry, for no man can serve God outside of His purposes! The best a man can do in this life is to accept the blood offering of His Son (which by the way, happened exactly on time) and commit his life to fulfilling the plans God has designed for his life. Anything else is vanity, an empty existence, for at the final Day of Judgment, only that which was done with the sanction of heaven will survive the purging fire of the Lord. Only the accomplished works that God had prepared for us to do will receive Divine approval.

Seek the Lord for the blueprint of *your* calling. Be patient to see how God will work out the details of your calling, and learn to wait on the Lord for its manifestation in due time.

The Timing of the Lord

Great temptations come with every generation. The excess in one generation is echoed by the rebellion of another. The challenge of waiting on the Lord has always been with us, but never like today. In a culture of "fast service" and "quick fixes," the temptation to hurry things has *never* been so strong. To be today's man of valor, you must win secret battles over your self and your culture by resisting the flurry of activity that seems to be a prerequisite for at least looking successful. Many men fall at this hurdle. Our culture today sells its merchandise with countless "buy now, pay later" schemes and continually tells us to treat ourselves with merchandise because "we're worth it." Placard waving protesters who march through the streets voicing their demands usually have the same chant at the end of their slogans. They all seem to sing together the words, "When do we want it? Now!" Do not succumb to the spirit of the age and do not allow your own soul to have everything it wants. Do not allow your children to have everything they want as soon as they want it. Teach them to wait. It's good for them. If your child is not made to wait when he is young, he will continue to demand things when he is older and his selfishness will create huge problems for many people.

People can put pressure on you to move ahead of God's timing. You will also have to deal with your *own* frustrations. Sometimes, you will want to move faster than God wants to. These pressures can present you with a subtle seduction of the ego that if yielded to will only guarantee ultimate disappointment. You must be careful. Sadly, in today's climate of rewards for results, the man of God in full time ministry is under great duress to continually initiate programs and ideas and sell them to the congregation as sure winners. There's nothing as tempting as quick, cost-effective results, both for the man himself and for the people he serves. Sometimes, its not the congregation he is serving that creates the pressure to get results fast, it is in fact, his *own* superiors! Whether from below or above, it all makes for a threatening atmosphere and the strains eventually take their toll.

Initiative certainly has merits, for where would we all be if God Himself had not loved us first and initiated the greatest enterprise of history in Jesus of Nazareth? But constantly *buying into* the latest dreams, ideas, and programs of Western culture is rarely in line with God's ways. If you yield to the temptation to give in to every selfish demand that promises quick results, it will produce nothing of lasting quality in the kingdom of God. Always hoping for a quick return will eventually cause deep depression as it becomes more and more apparent to you that contrary to the promises you feel God has made to you personally, you have been *busy going nowhere!*

It may be tough to have to admit that you have been building a "house on sand," using the knowledge and abilities of someone else, but the admittance will be liberating. Blessed is the man who truly knows how to *build in the Spirit* and who comprehends the meaning of the scripture that states:

Behold, I lay in Zion a stone for a foundation,
A tried stone, a precious cornerstone, a sure foundation;
Whoever believes will not act hastily.

—Isaiah 28:16

If you build in the perfect timing of God, you may pass through the "furnace of affliction" like Joseph in Egypt, but you will know by *experience* that the Lord has his perfect plan for everything. God is never agitated into activity. Happy is the man who can release himself from the expectations of carnal success and commit his soul "as unto a faithful Creator." That man will have learned to leave the results to God.

When God does decide to move, learn to wait for His optimum moment. Moses had to learn this lesson, when after forty years of waiting for God in the desert, he obeyed the call of God to go back to Egypt and tell

Pharaoh to "Let My people go!" Moses surprisingly discovered that things only got worse! The immediate results were horrendous. At that time, Moses asked the Lord the questions burning in his heart, but God only answered him at the optimum moment. God was waiting for the *Now* moment. Moses could do nothing until it was obtained.

"Now you will see what I will do to Pharaoh!" (Exodus 6 :1). That's the word, and that's the key. The power of God is seen in His actions and the perfection of God is seen in His timing. To the man who asks the same question as Moses, "Why is it that you have sent me?" the word of the Lord is, "Hold on!" Very soon God will act in His own way and more importantly, in His own time. The results are always magnificent, and they last forever!

Mandate to Mandate

If you want to be God's man of valor, you *must* wait on the Lord if you want true success. In Paul's qualifications for ministry in 2 Corinthians 6:4–10, patience heads the list! Before the apostle talks about needs and distresses, he speaks of the primary importance of patience. Patience is a necessary fruit, hidden in the "winters of delay," but gloriously developed when the "springtime of God's timing" ripens its skin. Happy is the man of God who knows who is in charge of the fruit of the earth. God Himself is the Lord of the Harvest, and if you truly understand that truth, you will learn to walk hand in hand with the "Author and Finisher" of your faith.

If you learn to "possess your soul in patience," and to rule your own spirit, God will be able to open doors of opportunity for you with incredible ease (Luke 21:19). You will discover that you are always the right man for the job. Your head will "lack no oil," because heaven is behind you as you bring the purposes of God into the world (Eccles. 9:8). Your only major concern will be in *"keeping your garments white"* as you travel through this dirty world (v. 8).

The Lord has designed your life to be built into a "holy temple," one brick at a time. The keys to spiritual growth are found within the Scriptures. The prophet Isaiah said that the Lord would build the people "precept upon precept, line upon line" (Isa. 28:10). The word *precept* means a directive or *mandate*, and the word *line* denotes a measure or *rule* of authority. Little by little, God builds up the spiritual life of His "chosen vessels." From time to time, according to a man's obedient fulfillment of God's plans, He will extend the borders of his ministry through the vehicle of a new mandate.

To be a "mighty man of valor," you must prove yourself faithful in the hidden matters of the heart. Make yourself available to God so that He can progressively enlarge the rule of authority in your life. The key to overcoming is the fulfilling of the purposes of God for your life, mandate to mandate. A *mandate* is a directive that comes from the hand of a superior. Authority supports it. When God opens a new chapter in a man's ministry, that new opportunity is a mandate from the hand of the Lord. It is charged with the power of God. Heaven stands in ratified agreement to reinforce the outworking of the commission being *"handed down."*

The Word that is sent by God never returns empty, but prospers in its mission to the place it was sent. Oh, the joy of having the wind of God behind you! Nothing can stop you in these moments. The thrill of running with a new mandate is exhilarating.

Most of the time, a new mandate will come when the old one has been fully accomplished or is at least, in its closing stages. When John the Baptist knew that the "sun was setting" on his life and ministry, he had the good sense to know that he must decrease so that the next Man could increase (John 3:30). Someone else was coming Who was greater than he, and this next Man was carrying a greater mandate! Into the cupped hands of John, the water of repentance was given to prepare the people of God. But into the open hands of Jesus, the nails of full atonement were given to save the people of God.

Oh that men, particularly older men of God, would understand their times and not be foolish in the last days of their ministries. Many an older minister has resisted the outworking of a younger man's mandate from the Lord. Believing they would remain in their long held positions forever, they failed to "number their days with wisdom." (See Psalm 90:12.) Through fear and selfishness, older men have caused great levels of stress among their "sons in the gospel." (See Philippians 2:22.) There was a pastor in England who served the Lord faithfully in the one church for over fifty years. During his years of ministry, God gave him many young men to help in the work. These young men took every opportunity to assist in the local church but were usually given the smallest of tasks. Rarely, if ever did they receive an opportunity to develop their speaking ministry. It seemed that the pulpit was out of bounds to them. When some of them began to take opportunities outside that local church, the pastor became angry and put a stop to their traveling ministries. Eventually, these young men left that local church one by one and when the pastor and his wife reached retirement age, there were sadly no competent men to take up the challenge. The pastor eventually died and the work faded away. Oh that present day leadership would always have one eye on the next generation! If they could possess the wisdom of John the Baptist, not only would they see the next generation develop in its calling, but they would also have an opportunity to sow into it. Then, even when they have left the field of battle, their works would follow them. Each man can only stand in the generation in which God has put them, but a life that has been totally engaged in the purposes of God can leave a legacy for subsequent generations, bringing to life the scripture that says: "...he being dead still speaks" (Heb. 11:4).

The man of valor must leave the scene of time, but his life, his example and his words can continue to shape the hearts and minds of generations to come.

CHAPTER FIVE
KEEPING THE COVENANT

As we return to the story of Gideon, we see that our man Gideon, whose heart had been "strangely warmed" by his unusual visitor that day, had begun to discern the supernatural element of this man's words. The words were already changing the atmosphere. A sense of heavenly commission now permeated the air around Gideon. Into the hand of Gideon, a mandate from God was beginning to form like a sword, and an edict from heaven was about to be revealed. Without hesitation, Gideon asks for a confirmation of the authenticity of this visitor's message.

JUDGES 6:17-24

17. Then he said to Him, "If now I have found favor in Your sight, then show me a sign that it is You who talk with me. 18. Do not depart from here, I pray, until I come

*to You and bring out my offering and set it before You."
And He said, "I will wait until you come back."*

19. So Gideon went in and prepared a young goat, and unleavened bread from an ephah of flour. The meat he put in a basket, and he put the broth in a pot; and he brought them out to Him under the terebinth tree and presented them. 20. The Angel of God said to him, "Take the meat and the unleavened bread and lay them on this rock, and pour out the broth." And he did so.

21. Then the Angel of the LORD put out the end of the staff that was in His hand, and touched the meat and the unleavened bread; and fire rose out of the rock and consumed the meat and the unleavened bread. And the Angel of the LORD departed out of his sight. 22. Now Gideon perceived that He was the Angel of the LORD. So Gideon said, "Alas, O Lord GOD! For I have seen the Angel of the LORD face to face."

23. Then the LORD said to him, "Peace be with you; do not fear, you shall not die." 24. So Gideon built an altar there to the LORD, and called it The-Lord-Is-Peace. To this day it is still in Ophrah of the Abiezrites.

What takes place in this section is probably the most important event in the whole story of the conflict with Midian. Indeed, one of the most important principles of ministry, especially world missions, is the issue of Covenant. It is the "blood of the Covenant" that brings peace with God. Nothing of Divine benevolence is going to happen within any community if God Himself is not seeking their peace and restoration.

Gideon knew just like every other man in Israel that their nation's uniqueness relied on the covenant that God had made with them. It had been the sacrifice of an innocent animal that initiated that agreement when they came out of Egypt. Gideon asked the stranger to stay, while he prepared a meal for him that was almost typical of the Lord's Passover in Egypt—a slaughtered young animal, unleavened bread, and broth.

He brought it out and presented it as a meal for the stranger to eat, but was told to lay everything out upon a nearby rock. Then he was told to pour out the broth upon the bread and meat. The angel of the Lord was about to turn the meal into a communion service! This natural, nearby rock had just become the table of the Lord. As the staff of God's authority touched the offering, the fire of God's acceptance leapt upwards out of the rock and consumed the sacrifice on its way back to heaven!

At that very moment, the stranger disappeared. He moved out of sight, yet not out of the scene. Gideon was struck with horror, fearing his own life because he had just seen what was now obvious to him—the Angel of the Lord—face to face! Panic gripped him, but the invisible Lord spoke into Gideon's heart saying, *"Peace be with you; do not fear, you shall not die"* (v. 23).

Peace with God had now been resumed. As far as Heaven was concerned, it was now *business as usual.* Through this man Gideon, the Lord had accepted his offering and restored the covenant of peace with Israel. A new day had come because a new altar of consecration had been erected. The name of the altar was called *Jehovah-*

shalom. From this man Gideon and his altar of peace, blessings would now return to Israel.

All this was possible because the God of Israel was, and still is today, a covenant-keeping God! Through one man's obedience, many would now be blessed.

This story reminds us of the Lord Jesus who was given as a "Covenant for the people." Through the offering of himself, many have come to know *eternal* peace with God. As an infant, Jesus revealed the purpose of his life when, over Bethlehem's fields on the night He was born, angels praised God saying, "Glory to God in the highest, and on earth peace, goodwill toward men" (Luke 2:14).

In the *advent* of Jesus, God's common grace appeared to all men with the prospect of eternal peace with God. But at the *ascension* of Jesus after the completion of His work and the acceptance of His offering on Calvary, the cry from the throne from that moment was, "Whosoever will may come!" In Christ's crucifixion, the peace offering upon Gideon's rock had found its full expression. Indeed, all blood sacrifices had now been eternally realized on the rock of Golgotha, where even death had to give way to the blood offering of the Prince of Life. The Lord Himself became the bread and wine, and even today, like the two travelers on the road to Emmaus, we can find Him in the covenant meal. He can move out of sight, but not out of the scene, for He is always with us, just like He was with Gideon.

What Do These Things Mean?

After Gideon presented his acceptable offering to God and raised an "altar of peace," he was then ready to proceed with the work. We too must learn these lessons, for as men of God, our ministries are not only under the common grace of God, but also under the saving grace of the Lord Jesus. God is the author of everything that is good. People throughout the ages have enjoyed the goodness of God in that He has given *"rain from heaven and fruitful seasons, filling their hearts with food and gladness"* (Acts 14:17). These common blessings have been given to us all from a benevolent God who loves the whole world. The apostle Paul told us that God has set time limits upon mankind *"so that they should seek the Lord, in the hope that they might grope for Him and find Him, though He is not far from each one"* (Acts 16:27). The heart of God the Father yearns for every *son of Adam* to repent and find his way back home. The goodness of God can be clearly seen in every generation, but there is an even deeper work that God is doing in the world. He is gathering to Himself, a *"chosen generation, a royal priesthood, a holy nation, His own special people"* (1 Peter 2:9). In every age, there are people whom God actively seeks out! His Holy Spirit is searching the world for His chosen ones. James calls these people *"the precious fruit of the earth"* (James 5:7). This work of the Holy Spirit is under the direct command of God to bring the people of God into a saving knowledge of the grace of the Lord Jesus Christ.

In our work for God, we must clearly understand that it's not a case of saying, "There's the world—let's go!" Rather, it is a case of saying, "Lord, what do you want me to do? Where do you want to send me? When do you want me to do it?" The Holy Spirit is the Spirit of missions, and it is He who governs all the work of God in your life. As in Gideon's case, from the personal altar experience onward, the Holy Spirit will begin to take control of your life. Having secured your individual obedience, you will be sent out into the field at the Holy Spirit's command. He will do the sending. He will open the doors.

The Spirit will send you to some places and stop you from going to others! That is why prophetic revelation is so important in your life and ministry. It can confirm your way and give you understanding as to what the mind of the Lord is.

Whenever we are engaged in missions, or attempt any work for God, we must ask Him what our role is in prayerful intercession. It is through the vehicle of prayer that God responds to change a situation. The big question is: "Can we find a place of favor with God where He will accept and allow intercession to be made?" Thankfully for us, there is a Man in heaven called *Jesus* who is a willing mediator between God and man. If requests are made in His Name, they always receive the consideration of the One who sits upon the throne because of the covenant He made with us *through* this Man.

The Lord Jesus was the maker of this new covenant, but we, like Gideon, need to be the *keepers of the covenant.* Our work is to plead with God for His forgiveness and ask for blessings upon the people we are reaching out to. Vital conversations must take place between the Lord and us before we launch out and sally forth into battle. We must not be afraid to ask some difficult questions, and we must not close our ears to the replies we receive. Before we do anything, we must first reverently ask these questions: "Lord, what do You want to do here? How do You want me to pray? Do You want me to pray for them at this time? Do You want me to establish Your covenant of peace with them? Have they committed offences against You that must be addressed? Will your Holy Spirit bring repentance to them? Are there any covenants and alliances made amongst them that have been broken? Are there any curses that have legal grounds to be working against them?"

Time—Another Dimension

I well remember a revelation the Lord gave to me concerning my work in East Germany. Near the city of Berlin, there is a large town where I was stationed. As I began to pray for the community, I saw in my heart and mind a strange picture. I saw an eagle flying with a snake in its claws. The word "Shame" seemed to cover the whole scene.

On my next visit to that city, I shared this revelation with a couple of intercessors that lived there and prayed for the area regularly. At that time, they couldn't directly relate to the vision, but kept the thoughts in their hearts. Upon my return a few months later, one of those intercessors showed me something very illuminating. She showed me some old newspaper clippings with photographs that showed a certain area of the town during the Second World War. She had some old pictures of the Heinkel Aircraft Production Company used by the Nazis during those times, and right above the front door, on top of the entrance was a huge black eagle, with a snake in its claws!

The aircraft from this factory had been the instruments of war that bombed countless civilians out of their homes and caused great loss of life. The buildings were now gone, but the shame was still there! Spiritual things do not bow to time. They travel through the generations, and they can have a lasting effect upon the life of a community for good or bad.

Things that are evil might not bow to time, but they will bow to the name of Jesus! Whatever the discord of human suffering that permeates a society, the voice of the Lord's blood speaks louder. The *"covenant of salt"* that the Lord Jesus made for us is eternal, and time must bow to the eternal. The Cross can bring life to any community, no matter how steeped in sin, and bring that community into harmony with God and His ways. We need help in our ministry to see as He sees, and through revelation and repentance, bring peace between God and the people.

Isn't this what the Bible describes as the ministry of the priest—to stand between God and the people, to make intercession for the transgressors, and to bring them into a place of acceptance with Him? Truly, the man who would dare to travel on missions with the Lord will know this priestly principle well. God will make his prayers prevail as he stands between the living and the spiritually dead. (See - Numbers 16:47,48)

The Scarlet Robe

When the Lord has confirmed His benediction on all your offerings of prayer, it is reasonable to assume that God wants to do something, and that He wants to do something through you! This moment of realization now becomes central to the whole matter. God wants to do something through you!

To you has now been given the opportunity to bring the kingdom of God into a community. If you have been privately responsive to Him, He will have all the tools He needs to get the job done. Having built in your heart an altar to His name through your obedience, He will want to show Himself strong on your behalf. The Lord is now with you to conquer.

Throughout the whole process, unknown to anyone but yourself, you will have been given a *spiritual* gift from God. It is a *"scarlet robe,"* and it fits you perfectly! Upon the breast pocket of that robe are the words, *"Endure all things."* Upon the sleeves on both arms is written, *"For the sake of God's elect."* This invisible coat now becomes your secret possession, for in a very real way, as well as figuratively, this *mantle of ministry* is what gives you a supernatural element to your work. Your willingness to suffer and endure afflictions for the Gospel's sake will now determine your true success. Heaven will not measure you by outward results, but by secret obedience in the crisis times of your life and ministry. These are the times when like Jesus in the garden of Gethsemane, you settle the issues with your obedience to God's perfect will. Decisions in moments like these cut deep into the heart. Nobody is around to see your struggle, but heaven is watching your every move because so much depends upon the outcome! True, the price of sin has been paid by Jesus, but *you* must also know how to wear the blood-red coat of the Great Commission.

In the very beginning of mankind, we saw how God had innocent creatures killed, so that their blood-red coats would cover our first parents' shame. For Adam, the first son of God on this earth, there was a covering. Years later, a special child called Isaac was born. He was the first son born supernaturally, and when his father Abraham was ready to offer him back to God, there was the provision of a ram to take his sacrificial place. But for Jesus, the eternal Son of God, He *was* the Lamb. He was the sacrifice, and He was the covering. Through His own blood, the wounded Savior built the great "altar of Bethel" and opened the very gate to heaven (Genesis 28:17). We must now walk in His steps. There is an altar experience waiting for all of us that will require us to put on the scarlet robe of the Gospel and identify ourselves with Him, being willing to share the reproach and rejection of this world. The Lord through His suffering brought in redemption, and we through our obedience bring in reconciliation.

There are some characteristics to the ministry of a man of valor, which include:

> To willingly suffer for the Gospels' sake.
> To be a good soldier and endure the afflictions of the Gospel according to the will of God.
> To reign in life through Christ Jesus, putting down all disobedient authorities once his own obedience has been fulfilled.

This is not a hidden thing with God, for the New Testament openly teaches us through the apostles that personal suffering for the will of God is as much a part of our experience as accomplishing great things.

"For to you it has been granted on behalf of Christ, not only to believe in Him, but also to suffer for His sake" (Philippians 1:29).

There was no hidden agenda when the Lord abruptly introduced Himself to Saul of Tarsus on the Damascus road. He brought him into the realities of ministry very quickly. After three days of blindness and no food nor drink, the Lord sent Ananias to heal Paul. Then Ananias began to tell Paul the truth about his life and calling. He would indeed accomplish great things by carrying the Lord's name to the Gentiles, to kings, and to the children of Israel, but he would also suffer in the process. God made him of strong character. This beloved man, whom we call the apostle Paul became fearless in these matters and even embraced the pain because he quickly learned the *"secret"* of the Lord. While death was working in him, life was being imparted to others. His testimony is found in these words:

"We are hard pressed on every side, yet not crushed; we are perplexed, but not in despair; persecuted, but not forsaken; struck down, but not destroyed—always carrying about in the body the dying of the Lord Jesus, that the life of Jesus also may be manifested in our body. For we who live are always delivered to death for Jesus' sake, that the life of Jesus also may be manifested in our mortal flesh, So then death is working in us, but life in you."

—2 Corinthians 4:8–12

Paul was not afraid to don the scarlet robe of personal cost. He had in his lifetime resisted sin even to the drawing of his own blood. He followed his Master, and just like Jesus, Paul's own vesture was *"dipped in blood."* Quite clearly, the ministry of Christ is not a career choice—it is the high calling of God! This is the way things are! God has made it so! The Gospel is free to the hearer, but expensive to the one who brings it. Like Joseph in those iron fetters, sometimes, under the wisdom of God, the *"beautiful feet that bring good news"* are hurt in the process. The time for garlands will come, but for today, true ministry requires a thorn.

Many years ago, I climbed a high hill in England to spend some time with God. It was a beautiful English setting, for the hill was full of trees, and the rays of an August sun punctured the floor of the forest. At the foot of the hill lay the thirteenth-century ruins of a priory, which gave its name to the location.

I was climbing the hill called *Mount Grace*. Upon reaching the halfway point, I stopped for a rest because the way up was steep. Then I proceeded to climb the rest of the way. Finding a spot on the top of the hill, I sat down and surveyed the scenery for miles. What a sight! The beautiful landscape of the North Yorkshire countryside, plus the added bonus of seeing British air force jets do their exercises high over the fields at unbelievable speed, was a treat.

Sitting there on a bed of purple heather, I plucked a piece of this tiny little flower and somehow knew that God was offering me a gift. Heather is such a small flower, but when it grows in profusion, it makes a royal carpet for miles around. Holding the flower in my hand, I then looked at the bright yellow-flowered, prickly gorse bushes around me. I heard the Lord's voice speaking to me saying, "It's time to pick the thorn now." I had so much difficulty tearing off a thorn from those evergreen shrubs that it punctured my hand and caused it to bleed. With the prospect of awkwardly getting down the steep hill, I left the thorn where I found it. I took the heather for a memento of the day, and I committed to memory the lesson of the thorn. In the days that lay ahead, the thorn played out its part in my life. Although the times were tough, the thought of the heather kept me going. I also found hidden in the lining of my own *spiritual* scarlet robe the words, *"light affliction—which is but for a moment."*

Peace Upon Israel

Gideon had brought peace upon Israel, and the work was soon to begin. God had showed once again that He is in control. He is the God who shows mercy. Revival and harvest are always God's prerogatives. Revival is never solely a case of men putting the laws of faith into action or forcefully appropriating the promises. Invariably, revival begins with God, the God who shows mercy. The laws of faith are put into action after God has released His word and the Spirit begins to breathe upon the promises planted long ago in people's hearts.

The man of God understands that this is God's order—the Lord must go before him! Just like king David experienced many years ago, the *"mulberry trees must stir"* (2 Samuel 5:24) before he goes out to war. Sadly, these principles of life have become a foreign language to many in the church today, because these principles fly in the face of the result-oriented society the Western world has become. The business world's idea of success in measured results cannot find a place in this kind of economy, for the business world's wisdom is not from above, but from the world of men.

The challenge to you as a man of valor is that you must walk between these two worlds. Suffering often begins at this point, for when you are expected to perform and get positive results, the Lord can make your current experiences take you in the opposite direction!

What ever job the Western man does in this present age, there are tremendous strains upon him to produce *"the numbers."* Sadly, Christian ministry has fallen prey to this obsession with progression! Week in and week out, it seems that the only thing that's really important to the senior leadership of some churches are *"the numbers."*

The demand for measurable success is heavy and the man who can't produce it will suffer. Anyone who wants to do Christian ministry today will find that there will be enormous pressure upon them to install programs in order to guarantee growth. However, the man of God will know instinctively that the Holy Spirit will not bless the mechanized apparatus of men. A *flash in the pan* might satisfy some for a moment, but the true man of God wants real gold. He wants the precious things that last forever and he is prepared to *wait* for it!

The Holy Spirit will look to such a man as this. He will always countenance the man who has refused the wisdom of this world and who has waited to move in the dynamics of God's River. The River of God will take you where He wants you to go and He will get you every place you need to be. He will also get you there in the His perfect timing. How can you not minister *life* to those who hear you when all these elements of God's River are in order? Will you be that man? Will you deliver yourself from not only the expectations of others, but even those expectations you put on yourself? So many young pastors come out of Bible College to take up a pastorate and they secretly think to themselves, "Ah! In so many months, years etc, I will have so many people in my church!" These pastors think they can measure their success by the amount of personal effort coupled with the amount of time that they have served their community. Young men like this "*fall at the first hurdle.*" This kind of thinking is understandable, because from a child, these young men have *gone up a grade* after every year of school study! Added to that are the outward ladders of success which men in ministry are measured by in their respective Fellowships, and when the expectation of yearly progress hasn't been achieved, they wrongly conclude that they must not have a call. They feel like a failure.

Let us not confuse the ways of the world with the principles of the kingdom. The job of any man of God is simply this – to remain in the River of God and minister *life!* The results can wait for Judgment Day. No man is going to impact the world for God without God! True success does not come from effort, even if it's meant for God. Success in God comes from believing His promises and walking in the Spirit. Some people call it *destiny*; some people call it *grace*. It's both of those things put together.

Gideon now stood in the River of God's purposes. It was to be a night that would change everything for him, his family and his nation.

CHAPTER SIX
BREAKING THE CHAINS

I n this section of our story, Gideon is now ready to conduct himself like a man should. He has entered adulthood and he is now taking responsibility for his own actions. The Lord stood poised and ready to use his "man of valor." However, before Gideon endeavors to bring victory to others, he must obtain personal victory on a domestic level.

Down through the years, many parents have said to their children, "You can't go out until your homework's done!" Gideon was about to emerge on the scene as the one who would bring salvation to Israel, but before he could go out, there was "homework" to be done! Gideon stood at the crossroads of decision in God's purposes. It was to be a night that changed everything for him, his family, and his nation.

JUDGES 6 :25-32

25. Now it came to pass the same night that the LORD *said to him, "Take your father's young bull, the second bull of seven years old, and tear down the altar of Baal that your father has, and cut down the wooden image that is beside it; 26. and build an altar to the* LORD *your God on top of this rock in the proper arrangement, and take the second bull and offer a burnt sacrifice with the wood of the image which you shall cut down."*

27. So Gideon took ten men from among his servants and did as the Lord had said to him. But because he feared his father's household and the men of the city too much to do it by day, he did it by night.

28. And when the men of the city arose early in the morning, there was the altar of Baal, torn down; and the wooden image that was beside it was cut down, and the second bull was being offered on the altar which had been built. 29. So they said to one another, "Who has done this thing?" And when they had inquired and asked, they said, "Gideon the son of Joash has done this thing." 30. Then the men of the city said to Joash, "Bring out your son, that he may die, because he has torn down the altar of Baal, and because he has cut down the wooden image that was beside it."

31. But Joash said to all who stood against him, "Would you plead for Baal? Would you save him? Let the one who would plead for him be put to death by morning! If he is a god, let him plead for himself, because his altar has been torn down!" 32. Therefore on that day he called him

Jerubbaal, saying, "Let Baal plead against him, because he has torn down his altar."

That night, the Lord gave Gideon instructions concerning the altar of Baal that was on his father's property! How sad that a man like Gideon's father would diminish his nobility by having an altar to a false god on his land. The apostasy of the nation had become great. Jehovah, the one true God, had been largely forgotten. The people had turned to false gods. And to add insult to injury, any one that raised a voice against Baal would be subjected to grievous consequences.

There had been a time in the not-so-distant past when all worshipers of foreign gods would have been put to the sword and their town left in a burnt-out ruinous heap. The times however had changed, and now Gideon had to stand up for God, and make courageous decisions that would make him a mighty man of valor. His decisions that night would begin the process of victory by first breaking the chains of bondage in his own family to the false god Baal.

A Few Good Men

Obeying the word of the Lord, Gideon took ten good men with him to help, and set off that night to do what was possibly one of the hardest things he would ever have to do in his life. Whatever his relationship had been with his father, from this night onward it would be different. His father was spiritually lost in idolatry, and this night was the night when his father's idolatrous headship was going to be broken off Gideon's life. The bondage brought into the family through his father's apostasy must now be broken, and his father's headship must now cease to control Gideon's experience. As God's man of valor, Gideon must learn quickly that the kingdom of God will come first *to* him before it comes *through* him to his family and to his nation.

Afraid of breaking down the altar of Baal during the daytime, Gideon and his companions waited for the night. Under the cover of darkness, they broke down the altar of Baal, cut down the wooden idol, and offered a seven-year-old bullock on the rock that God had so wonderfully accepted his previous, personal offering.

The Midianites had cruelly oppressed the nation of Israel for seven years. Now, in the darkness of the night, a bullock that was seven years old was being offered by fire unto the Lord. The blood poured forth, the fire leapt toward heaven, and the rock of God's altar silently witnessed its testimony of a peace offering to the Lord of heaven and earth. Gideon and his ten men went home and waited for the day to begin.

"Who Has Done This Thing?"

The sun of a new day shone its first rays upon the town, and very soon, the crescendo of frightened, angry voices pierced the air: "Who has done this?" Panic and rage spilled over into a public outcry that eventually led the people to the gate of Gideon's home. The "word on the street" had clearly indicated that Gideon was responsible for the outrageous thing that had happened in the night.

The people shouted angrily to Gideon's father: "Bring out your son that he may die!" Obeying the word of the Lord had thrust Gideon into deep trouble, and now his very life hung in the balance.

Public rage is not an uncommon thing in working for the kingdom. Many times, obeying the Word of the Lord will not endear you to a community of people. At times, it can cause the people who witness your obedience to God to become enraged. The example of the early apostles during the days of expansion of the early church will show this to be true, for entire cities were inflamed with their preaching. For every missionary, there is always a risk of disturbing the peace when engaged in the Gospel, because the powers of darkness are afraid they will lose their hold over their victims. They are afraid that they will lose their place.

When John Wesley visited the many towns and villages in England, it was a common experience for mobs to meet him and chase him and his friends out of the area! Some times they even attempted to kill him! In moments like these, it becomes abundantly clear that the "strong man" becomes very upset when his goods are being taken! (Matthew 12:29).

The apostle Paul had similar experiences when entire stadiums, filled with frightened angry people, clamored to have him instantly killed. And they would have been successful had not God intervened! This was also the Lord Jesus' experience when he visited his hometown of Nazareth. When he spoke to them in the local synagogue, they became incensed with his message and they rose up against him. They would have thrown him to his death off a nearby cliff, but God intervened.

In our story, Gideon has now been thrown into a crisis. He could only lift his eyes toward heaven, for only heaven could save him at that moment. He had accomplished the task that the Lord had asked him to do, but he had become "public enemy number one" as a result! The breaking down of his father's idolatrous altar had provoked the spiritual "strong man" to murderous anger, because goods were about to be taken!

Family Ties—Apron Strings

There comes a time for every man of God when the family bond, whether good or bad, must be subdued to the authority of God. The natural authority of the parent must give way to the call of God and to the headship of the Lord upon his life. In the new day of God's authority upon a man, the "ties that bind" are the *first* things to be tested, for even maternal "apron strings" can be made of steel instead of cotton!

There is often a stubborn, prideful unwillingness in many parents to let go. Years of familiarity, coupled with responsibility, make it difficult for some parents to see the anointing of ministerial office upon their son. It's much easier to see the *boy* than to acknowledge the *man*, and the temptation to continue pulling rank over him is overwhelming at times.

This sad but seemingly inescapable scenario has surfaced at the beginning of ministry for many men.

King Solomon had to cut the "apron strings" with his mother, Bathsheba, when she tried to persuade Solomon to give Abishag the Shunammite woman to his brother Adonijah. (See 1 Kings 2:12-25). Solomon had naturally deferred to his mother in respect and positioned her to sit at his right hand, virtually promising her anything she asked of him. But when he perceived that she had become a vehicle of manipulation, he flatly refused her request. Furthermore, he had Adonijah executed for his guilt in being a pretender to the throne (1 Kings 2:25).

At the inception of his ministry, our Lord Jesus also faced a similar situation of "mother knows best." His own beloved mother, Mary, came to him at the wedding feast in Cana, and did what mothers have done so well for centuries—veiled a request in a seemingly innocuous statement. Jesus discerned the intention and in what was probably a difficult thing for him to do, he cut any "apron string" of ownership authority that was residual in the mind of his mother. "Woman," He replied to his mother, "what does your concern have to do with Me?" (John 2:4).

Throughout the hidden years of his life in Nazareth, Jesus had honored his parent's authority, but after the baptism in water by John, the anointing of the Messiah was upon his life in all its resplendent glory. The dove of the Holy Spirit was now the authority resting upon his head, and no family authority, however well intentioned, was in control of his life. However, at the wedding in Cana he graciously responded to his mother by meeting the need through a wonderful display of power.

73

That day, Jesus set into motion his miraculous ministry with a sign that he would give the wine of his own blood in the "hour to come." He turned water into wine and met his mother's request, but Mary never pushed her desires upon him after that. Many years earlier, Mary had received a similar warning when Jesus was about twelve years of age. The experience that day in Cana affirmed the things she had kept in her heart for years.

This experience is common to all anointed ministers of God. The family ties must be broken, even if they have been good ones. Not only that, but some family demons must be faced, too! How can a man of valor bring deliverance to others if he himself is bound by ancestral bondages that neither he nor his family can overcome? That is why the Lord will always bring a minister to an early crisis point concerning these matters. Like David, if you cannot kill the lion and the bear of private life, how can you slay the giant in the public arena?

Often the first spirits to attack a man of valor are those that have dominated his family and their forebears. Ancestral bondages wrapped up within his cultural upbringing would love to continue their hold upon his life, but he must defeat them. He must be ruthless with himself, being prepared to alter anything in his thoughts, habits, and disposition that are not in agreement with the Word of God.

"Homework" for the man of God is raising a new altar upon the rock of Christ Himself, and offering his service in accordance with God's Word. To become a man of valor, you must have a private encounter with the Great

74

High Priest whose Word is sharper than any two-edged sword and who can shine the light of God into the very depths of your soul. Like Joshua at the beginning of his ministry, you must be exposed to God's authority by seeing the drawn sword of the Lord, and thereafter walking on holy ground.

The battle for control in these personal areas is a fierce conflict, and deliverance requires so much willingness to change and so much courage to undertake it. Only heaven watches this battle. Public rewards will follow the conqueror at a later date.

Name-calling

Gideon's father stepped forward that day and, through the providence of God, rescued Gideon from a certain death. Whatever the murmuring among the angry crowd, one comment from Gideon's father, Joash, caused momentary derision to enter the entire mob: *"If Baal is a god, let him take vengeance himself on the one who has destroyed his altar."* (See Judges 6:31.) With that spoken, the crowd was strangely stilled, and that day Joash called his son *Jerubbaal* as an invitation to Baal to avenge himself for the breaking down of his altar.

Ordinarily, names from fathers had a tendency to endure in time and in power, but on this occasion it seems that Gideon, though named *Jerubbaal*, had broken his father's dark authority. After throwing down his altar the previous night, Gideon stepped into a new authority and was now "his own man." And so, for every man of valor who has successfully broken the chains of darkness over his life, no amount of name-calling nor other negative words will have any power over him. He is free, free indeed!

CHAPTER SEVEN
CROSSING THE LINE

The moment had arrived. The next few hours would prove to be decisive for Gideon and the Midianite forces. The enemy had come with huge numbers into the land like a flood, but the Lord was going to raise the battle flag of warfare against *them!* For seven years, God had allowed the enemy to enter into the land to destroy it, but this would prove to be their last assault. They were about to cross the line of God's permission, and that could only mean judgment for them. The Lord had hidden from them the thing He was about to do.

JUDGES 6: 33-35

33.Then all the Midianites and Amalekites, the people of the East, gathered together; and they crossed over and encamped in the Valley of Jezreel. 34. But the Spirit of the LORD came upon Gideon; then he blew the trumpet, and the Abiezrites gathered behind him. 35. And he sent messengers throughout all Manasseh, who also gathered behind him. He also sent messengers to Asher, Zebulun, and Naphtali; and they came up to meet them.

The great disadvantage of all enemies of God lies in the fact that they never know what He is doing. Everything He does is done out of the hidden wisdom of His heart, and it is often interpreted as foolishness by this present world.

Indeed, the apostle Paul told the early believers that if the princes of this world knew what God was doing in Jesus of Nazareth, they would not have crucified the Lord of glory. The rulers of this fallen world can only see what God has in mind after the events have already taken place! God is in charge – of everything! (1 Cor 2:8).

This lack of light and understanding is the beginning of God's judgment upon them. But for those who are on the Lord's side, the wisdom of God is dispensed to give them necessary insight. Those fighting the Lord's battles are always a step ahead of the enemy because of the military intelligence they receive by the Spirit of God. Before fire rained down on Sodom and Gomorrah and caught the inhabitants unaware, the Lord had revealed to Abraham and his family what He was about to do. Before the old world was taken in a deluge, Noah and his family were told what to do to escape.

In our story of Gideon, just like the Pharaoh of Egypt who came hurtling to his death in the Red Sea, so the children of the East swarmed upon the land of Israel only to find themselves trapped in the valley of God's judgment.

With invisible hooks in their jaws, and drawn by their own hearts' lust for conquest, they were corralled into the pen of the Lord's displeasure. They looked invincible by their sheer numbers, and being without equal in their strength, they encamped in the valley, fearing nothing. Little did they realize that this valley of Jezreel, later named *Megiddo*, was for them the judgment seat of God. On this day of battle, the events surrounding the Midianites would point to another day of great slaughter in the future when the conflict of the ages would finally take place.

Bricks Without Straw

The enemy had crossed the line, and God was going to respond. Like so many nations before and after, the Midianites had been used by God to punish Israel. But they would be punished even more severely themselves when the time appointed had come. The Lord had decreed seven years of punishment for His people because of their disobedience. Seven years had been accomplished, and to continue destroying Israel beyond the decree was to cross the line of God's permission. By entering into the land again, the Midianites caused the Spirit of God to signal a call to action. Not only had they entered into the land again, they had already begun to slay many people in Tabor, some of whom were in close relationship to Gideon!

Here is another lesson in spiritual warfare: God allows the enemy to do his work—but only for so long. Because the heart of evil knows little restraint, it's only a matter of time before the line is crossed. When the enemy begins to add insult to injury, God has the basis for initiating righteous war.

The whole ministry of Samson is based upon this premise. His supernatural endowment of power came upon him *after* the enemy had committed the first offence! (See Judges 16.) God's works are always justified, and so just as He did in Samson's life, He will seek an occasion against the enemy before His judgment is unleashed. Time and time again, the Spirit came upon Samson in response to the offences done against him.

For us as God's people, this principle means that sometimes in the field of the Lord's service we must be offended first. The afflictions of the Gospel require that on some occasions, we must be bruised first in order for the enemy to cross over the line. Not only will the work of God be difficult at times, personal hardship can be increased by unreasonable authorities who in their anger towards you will force you into a position of making "bricks without straw." Like the children of Israel in Egypt, you will have to *possess your soul in patience* and allow the enemy to cross over the line, because once that's done, the Lord will move in quickly.

"Now you shall see what I will do to Pharaoh," said the Lord to Moses (Exod. 6:1). By making things worse for the children of Israel, Pharaoh had ripened himself for judgment and filled up his sins to the boiling point. This ripening for judgment rarely, if ever, happens over night because the Lord is "merciful and gracious, longsuffering, and abounding in goodness and truth" (Exod. 34:6). But when the sins of a people have gone full term, the sword of the Lord is unsheathed, and war is declared!

The man of valor must not be surprised if the enemy goes further than what was anticipated. Any "late in the day" unexpected blow should not come as a complete shock, and any battle fatigue that causes a gradual weakening of his position should not discourage God's man to the point of giving up. At the bottom of the whole experience he will find a small, spiritual key that will dispel the ominous clouds of depression and put a song of praise in his heart. Picking up the "key of wisdom" out of the dust and holding it up to the only ray of light available, he will find the answer to his situation. Imprinted on the key, through tearful eyes he will read the words: *"When I am weak, then I am strong"* (2 Cor. 12:10).

Although small in size, amazingly that little key opens a huge door that was hidden behind him, albeit there all the time. Turning the lock, the hinges swing the door into the blue brightness of a brand new day! Looking back, over the portal of the great door he reads a name: *Jehovah-Jireh.* God's provision for the hour at hand can now be seen as he walks through this door.

This door was the well of water for Hagar and her son, Ishmael, in the day of their affliction. This door was the sacrificial ram caught in the thicket for Abraham and his son, Isaac. And this door was the door that the apostle Paul went through on an almost daily basis! "...In deaths often," he added to his list of service! (2 Cor. 11:23). The apostle Paul had made the transition between the garment of the flesh and the mantle of the Spirit to the point that he gladly endured affliction of the most painful kind as long as the Spirit of Christ was resting upon him. The weaknesses he carried as a minister of Christ were his passport into the heavenly realms, and the infirmities he bore became his key to opening the door of Gods' provision, --

"as having nothing, and yet possessing all things" (2 Cor. 6:10).

In our story, Gideon now stood at this door. Faced with overwhelming odds in the natural realm, the decision that day to turn the key and go through, believing God's Word, would prepare him for another orbit. Beyond the door, there was a supernatural God waiting for him. In his mind he can hear the words that were spoken over his life: "The LORD is with you, mighty man of valor!"

The Blue Mantle

Stepping through the door of God's provision, Gideon took up his position on holy ground. Immediately, the Spirit of the Lord clothed Himself upon Gideon. In that moment, the heavenly blue mantle of the Spirit of God fell upon him. At once everything changed!

The Lord is a *Man of War,* and though the enemy was still in the valley in vast numbers, and the battle was still to be fought, the outcome from that moment forward was never in doubt—Midian was finished! The oppression was over. Peace with God had come to the nation.

Gideon arose as a mighty man of valor, and the first thing he did was to blow a trumpet call to assemble for war. From his lips there came a sound from heaven to all the neighboring tribes. All who heard the trumpet responded. This is characteristic of the Spirit of God coming upon a man. The enduing of the Spirit often causes that man to have a voice that rings of heaven. From his lips and out of his mouth there will flow the words of God, and all who hear it will respond in some way.

On a later day in the calendar of Israel, there would come a day when the Spirit of God would clothe Himself upon a crowd of people with wind and fire. Out of their lips there would come forth, authoritative words in many languages, and all who could hear would respond in some way. (See Acts 2.) The man who has the *voice of God* in his speech is the man who has the *rod of God* in his hand. Such a man has been commissioned to rule the battle of the Lord and to have the people of God follow his lead.

The response had been good that day in Israel. Gideon had done the reasonable thing by calling for help. There is nothing wrong with calling for help and doing the reasonable thing, unless the Lord says differently. Troops were needed. Troops were called for. But on this occasion, God intended to do things radically different!

Unbeknown to Gideon, the journey ahead was going to be full of surprises. It would end with cheers of victory, but in the most testing of ways to himself and his men. All Gideon knew for sure was that God was with him—

or did he know that? The mantle of the Spirit was upon him, the trumpet had been blown, and the people had responded, aligning themselves with his vision. But Gideon wanted more personal assurance from God. There was no hiding place for him now. It was not like before when he had other places to go.

Now he was well beyond the "tree-line of the mountain," and not only could everyone *see* him, they all wanted to *hear from him!* Thrust into the bright light of public gaze, he sought God for another private audience to settle his spirit. Gideon asked for more confirmations from God, and the Lord was gracious to him and granted his requests. The Lord was happy to confirm that He was in control of the entire situation, and to confirm that Gideon was *His choice.* Laying a fleece of wool on the floor, Gideon received the message loud and clear when, after two consecutive nights, God had alternated the dew upon the fleece and the ground to leave him filled with confidence for the task ahead.

God would soon teach Gideon a most important lesson, one that all who would work for Him must learn. It is this: One man *with God* constitutes a majority! A big task lay ahead for Gideon, but that day he stood confirmed in his faith, focused in his vision, and empowered in his leadership.

Understanding this lesson of "one man with God" is fundamental for building a successful ministry over a lifetime. Whatever may befall the man of valor in the battlefields of life, as long as God is with him, everything will work out for the best. There are many treacherous paths upon which the man of God must walk and if it were not for the fact that God was indeed with him, he would probably fall victim to the wiles and snares of ungodly men.

When, along the path you've taken, the giant of "Unjust suffering" steps out of his den and strikes you with his club, it will be hard to see the Lord's benevolent plans for your life. Like Joseph, who endured so much unfair treatment, you have to learn the vital lesson that what matters most is not the cruelty of men, nor even the hardheartedness of your brethren, but the fact that God is still with you! Only those without God fall to their destruction, but the "steps of a good man are ordered by the LORD" (Ps.37:23). This truth is the heart of ministry—you and God. Anything outside of that *"Emmanuel"* experience is secondary to the cause. Throughout history, mighty men of faith have expressed that "the best thing in life is having God with them in the work!"

Chapter Eight
The Economy of God

The Lord was indeed with Gideon. The victory was never in doubt, but a strange road lay ahead. The God of Israel would reveal to Gideon that He is *totally* in control of the whole situation. The Lord Himself began to direct the campaign, and the course to be undertaken would become a surprise to everyone! The wisdom of God was about to be revealed through some apparently foolish decisions his general, Gideon, would be caused to make.

JUDGES 7:1-8

1.Then Jerubbaal (that is, Gideon) and all the people who were with him rose early and encamped beside the well of Harod, so that the camp of the Midianites was on the north side of them by the hill of Moreh in the valley. 2. And the LORD said to Gideon, "The people who are with you are too many for Me to give the Midianites into their hands, lest Israel claim glory for itself against Me, saying, 'My own hand has saved me.' 3. Now therefore, proclaim in the hearing of the people, saying, 'Whoever is fearful and afraid, let him turn and depart at once from Mount Gilead.'" And twenty-two thousand of the people returned, and ten thousand remained.

4. But the LORD said to Gideon, "The people are still too many; bring them down to the water, and I will test them for you there. Then it will be, that of whom I say to you, 'This one shall go with you,' the same shall go with you; and of whomever I say to you, 'This one shall not go with you,' the same shall not go." 5. So he brought the people down to the water. And the LORD said to Gideon, "Everyone who laps from the water with his tongue, as a dog laps, you shall set apart by himself; likewise everyone who gets down on his knees to drink." 6. And the number of those who lapped, putting their hand to their mouth, was three hundred men; but all the rest of the people got down on their knees to drink water.

7. Then the LORD said to Gideon, "By the three hundred men who lapped I will save you, and deliver the Midianites into your hand. Let all the other people go, every man to his place." 8. So the people took provisions and their trumpets in their hands. And he sent away all the rest of Israel, every man to his tent, and retained those three hundred men.

Gideon needed to learn a cardinal principle of God's economics: *Faith and obedience are the currency of the kingdom.* So it is with *every* man of God. Somewhere along life's road, the Lord will teach him how to enter into the economy of God through *"giving up what he cannot keep, to gain what he cannot lose."* Heaven knows when a man has spending power with God, because that man has bought gold from the Lord in the crucible of obedient faith.

God initiated the beginning of Gideon's greatness by weakening his position so that he would learn that the way to the high places is through the valley. Like the greatest Man who ever lived, Gideon would first descend before he would ascend to be the head of all things. God's mighty man of valor was about to be offered another clothing experience.

Jesters' Clothing

After having identified himself with the scarlet robe of suffering, and having received the wonderful blue mantle of the Spirit's endowment of power, new clothes must be put on to triumph in the next hour. They are the clothes of a clown! Putting them on proves to be one of the most difficult things for *any* man of God, for they make him look foolish. There is absolutely no personal glory in them at all!

The scarlet robe of suffering has its honor, and the mantle of power has its admiration, but the jesters' clothes speak only of embarrassment and humiliation. No man wants to wear these loud, striped clothes. No man in his right mind wants to be figuratively shod with red, oversized boots that jingle when he walks, because no one wants to play the part of being the fool. For the man of high esteem, the last thing he wants is to appear before his peers with the jingly jester's cap on his head, looking like he's lost all good sense. He finds it excruciating, but that is where the secret to power lies. The word *excruciating* means "to crucify," and through the presentation of foolish weakness, the wisdom of God is made perfect.

Joshua had to figuratively wear these clothes when he led the children of Israel around the walls of Jericho without speaking a word. Naaman the Syrian captain symbolically wore these clothes when, at the prophet's command, he dipped himself into the river Jordan seven times for his healing. The apostle Paul wore these clothes on many an occasion as he stood before kings, nobles, and countrymen in chains, testifying to the world that he and the other apostles had become fools for Christ's sake.

The reward for wearing these garments is the victory of a job well done! The walls of opposition fall flat, the incurable are wonderfully healed, and as in Gideon's case, the enemy is routed in overwhelming defeat. Can you wear the "fool's cap" if required? Every man of God will at some time in his walk with the Lord appear foolish in his decisions. His very job description is viewed as foolish by the world because God has ordained that those who inherit eternal life will be saved by the foolishness of preaching! Added to that is the fact that the *natural* man cannot receive the things of God because they are foolishness to him! There will be times when you will just have to obey the *word* the Lord has spoken to you and carry it through, no matter how red your face might blush. For the man of God, there is no such thing as a *"door"* that's so small, he can't get through! Even the "eye of a needle" presents no problem for the man who can humble himself for the cause!

Hard for a Rich Man

For a man with leadership ability to give up the "driving seat" of his life, it requires a level of obedience that will test his character like nothing else. The very thought of abandoning the controls sends a shiver down his spine, because if he's not in control, then someone else is! The need to know everything, which ensnared man's first parents in the Garden, continues to dominate the hearts and minds of mankind. We have become as gods, because we want to know what's going on! If we know what's going on, we can make contingency plans and govern the outcome. We can minimize any damage along the way and prevent ourselves from looking foolish through silly mistakes, for what men fear the most is public disgrace.

The opinion and judgments of people affect us more than we are prepared to admit, and the fear of looking a failure becomes a hurdle that not many can jump. We crave the praise of people so much that to be viewed with disdain and portrayed as "the bad one" cripples our ability to make the right decision. For many, it's at this point where true failure actually takes place. They may continue on as if nothing has happened, but inside they know that they have secretly said *"No!"* to God. The successful man of God will be the one who can say, "I have finished the course." Such a man has never said

"*No*" to God at any stage of his life, and a crown awaits him in the life to come.

The man who will not abandon himself to the cross, will rarely see the power of God operating in his life. God will leave him to his own contingency plans. Grace will still remain, but victory will be limited, because great victories come with great sacrifice. Pivotal moments in history are made when men enter into the *"fiery furnace"* of sacrifice and hold their position knowing that there is no back door of escape! Total victory requires a man like Jesus of Nazareth, who, despising the public shame, abandoned himself to the will of God and the resultant pain of public crucifixion. In so doing, he accomplished the greatest achievement in the history of the world. The Lord's man of valor must also learn how to accept the reversals of God in his life so that greater things can be accomplished. The greater the degree of success a man enjoys, the harder it is to do this. The personal "armor" collected over years is difficult to take off, and to run light-footed into the battle becomes too risky.

It is hard for a man, rich in the treasures of biblical knowledge and ministry experience, to strip down to the bare minimum in order to pass through the "eye of the needle" gateway. Years of being built up in the Word can often block the way through into God's River of life. The apostle Paul would not allow this to happen in his life, and so it was with conviction that he counted all things as loss so that he might win Christ (Phil. 3:8). Paul was prepared to drop all his treasures of knowledge in order to get to know the Lord. Paul knew that although the

Holy Scriptures are the vehicle of life, he also knew that it is the Holy Spirit who gives life!

Every man of God is challenged with this "small door" of God's choosing, because it is God's gateway into the economics of the kingdom. Many leaders are challenged in this matter, only to find themselves too big and too armored to get through. They are unwilling to drop their weapons and lose their respect. When great challenges rise up and face them, they look for someone else to take the risk. Unfortunately for them, there always seems to be a young "David" who will put on the jesters' clothes of apparent foolishness and through the comedy of *"sling and stones"* change the course of history!

God—the Reducer

Gideon was about to enter the Hall of Fame. The Lord was going to deliver Israel through Gideon, but in the His own way. Knowing that deceitfulness is resident in every man's heart, the Lord chose a way that would bring glory to Himself and save the children of Israel from themselves. Making sure that Israel didn't become an enemy to God again through self-sufficient pride, He began to do the opposite of what men would naturally do. He began to take away from Gideon and the children of Israel their strength, bit by bit.

The diminishing of Israel's strength by degrees was vital to the outcome of the battle. Out of weakness, they were to become strong. This course of action, which would have failed approval in any military academy, turned into God's master strategy for the occasion. The tribes that had heard the trumpet message had gathered to Gideon in numbers. They assembled at the well of Harod, and the noise of prospective battle was rumbling in the crowd. But there seemed to be an echoing word of God whispering in the breeze that said, "Not by might nor by power, but by My Spirit, says the LORD" (Zech. 4:6).

Gideon immediately obeyed the Lord's command and embraced the decision to allow more than two thirds of his army to return home because they were frightened. The majority left, but it wasn't enough! More were to go!

Brought to the Water

Both Gideon and the children of Israel were now entering a critical moment in the campaign. God was about to bring them down to the waters for testing. Using criteria known only to the Lord, the God who knows all the hearts of men, separated only three hundred warriors to help Gideon fulfill his task.

This testing at the water was not without precedent. When Moses brought the children of Israel out of Egypt, God brought them to the point of testing. The people complained bitterly because of the lack of water. God brought water out of the rock, and called them *"the waters of Meribah,"* or "waters of strife." As the psalmist would later record, the Lord said, "I tested you at the waters of Meribah" (Ps. 81:7).

There's nothing quite like being in the public eye when everything seems to be going wrong. At such a time, messages about the *"abundant life"* seem hollow and irrelevant. Your experience is taking you down to the waters of testing. This can be a season of trial for any one in ministry, but it is especially arduous if you become a new church planter. To everyone who has had the courage to plant a new work, there comes this kind of trial. It happens to most, if not all, church planters in one way or another.

It also happens at a time when membership in the local church is declining. A rabbi friend of mine aptly called his experience of congregational downsizing, when many of his people felt "called" to leave than to stay, a *Gideon revival!*"

Someone beginning a new local church work in God today often finds himself in the same predicament as Moses did in his day, and with the same question of doubt ringing out: "Is the Lord among us or not?" This is the kind of trial the Lord endured when Satan tempted him to make bread out of stones. Jesus had a legitimate basic need that Satan exploited, just as the people had in Moses' day. They weren't asking for wealth—they were asking for water. When peoples' basic needs are not being met, even for a moment, the complaints arrive quickly.

Oh that we would learn from the Master, who, though having legitimate needs, chose to discipline himself through the moment and wait for God's timing. The man who will wait for God will have angels in attendance when the provision comes.

When times of testing come to a local church body, the blame for what is happening is always placed upon the leader. As a result, it creates a very difficult period of time for the pastor and his wife. Because such a test results in diminishing numbers, as it did with Gideon's men, some of the pastor's "best people" may leave. Some who have been with him from "day one" may have had their confidence in the work dashed. Others who transferred in from other church bodies may have had their idealism burst in light of the then, present realities. Not only are some of these people spiritual in their outlook, they are often faithful in their tithes to the Lord. As these tithing members leave, the momentary loss of income becomes an anxiety for the pastor and his wife to carry. Added to all this is the emotional upheaval caused as people in whom the pastor has invested time and emotion see fit to join another church, conveniently forgetting his sacrificial input into their lives. At such times as these, the man of God will do well to remember that God is *allowing* all these things to happen!

How this test from God is affecting the congregation is important, but the greater issue is how it is affecting the leader himself. Moses failed at these waters, and he was one of the greatest men who ever lived! What is the man of valor to do in this kind of situation? This season of painful reduction brings with it more questions than answers. The accompanying sense of abandonment and rejection can drown a leader in bitterness if he *allows* it.

The answer always rests in God. God's man must appropriate God's grace under fire. He must *hear* from heaven the encouragement so many earthly soldiers throughout history have heard from their superior officers in the heat of battle: "Steady boys, steady! Hold your position, Soldier! Today is not the day to lay down your weapons." In moments like these, the pastor must hold on. At all costs, he must *"hold the bridge"* and fulfill the mandate of, *"...having done all, to stand!"* (Eph. 6:13).

Sweeten the waters with forgiveness, and very soon you will hear a voice from above saying, "Come up higher!" Successfully passing through the waters of bitter disappointment constitutes a major personal victory. It becomes the platform for enduring reward. The Lord Himself will turn the season, and new growth will appear. You will be different. More importantly, the people you lead will be different. Your anointing to lead will be increased through the congregation's newfound willingness to serve you and your vision. The whole experience will have been a dark tunnel from which the kingdom of God has beautifully blossomed, but the personal scars, though healed, will remain. They will remain in this life to teach you and others the wonderful wisdom of God, and they will serve you in the life to come as marks of service for the Master.

Three Hundred Men

Three hundred men were separated to the ministry that day. Three hundred had successfully passed the test with God, and this small group, under the leadership of Gideon, was all that the Lord required. In reality, the Lord didn't even need these three hundred men, but I think He knew that Gideon needed them. God is so kind to us. He knows how weak we really are and that although He must take us to *"the edge"* some times, He still leaves us with a deposit of assurance to calm the nerves. The three hundred men took their food and their trumpets and remained with Gideon. While the rest returned homeward, Gideon's men watched the enemy beneath them in the valley.

Now the camp of Midian was below him in the valley.

Judges 7:8

Gideon and his three hundred men had something else in their favor in that they were positioned on higher ground. The enemies beneath were invincible in their own eyes and took little thought about their vulnerability in the valley. So it is with all nations that think they're safe from trouble. Security becomes a little more lax and carelessness pervades. Even a *Trojan horse* is treat like a gift of honor, because the thought of a surprise defeat is never in their minds. History reveals that most empires have been destroyed when former hardships and disciplines have given way to future generations living in ease. The comfort loving part of human nature has guaranteed this kind of outcome throughout the ages. Destruction was about to fall upon the Midianites. They were lying in the valley, largely at ease with themselves, fearing almost nothing. A cursory watch was put around their perimeters that evening but their fate was sealed.

CHAPTER NINE
STRENGTHENED BY THE PROPHETIC

fter Gideon's army of three hundred men had been selected, the Lord once again responded to obedience with immediate action. On the very day that Gideon took a step of faith by reducing his army to three hundred men, the Lord declared the victory! In the quiet breezes of the evening, the God of Israel spoke to his servant saying, "Arise, go down against the camp, for I have delivered it into your hand" (Judg. 7:9). All things were now ready for the battle ahead. The word of God had been spoken, and heaven stooped to conquer.

JUDGES 7:9-15

9. It happened on the same night that the LORD said to him, "Arise, go down against the camp, for I have delivered it into your hand. 10. But if you are afraid to go down, go down to the camp with Purah your servant, 11. and you shall hear what they say; and afterward your hands shall be strengthened to go down against the camp." Then he went down with Purah his servant to the outpost of the armed men who were in the camp. 12. Now the Midianites and Amalekites, all the people of the East, were lying in the valley as numerous as locusts; and their camels were without number, as the sand by the seashore in multitude.

13. And when Gideon had come, there was a man telling a dream to his companion. He said, "I have had a dream: To my surprise, a loaf of barley bread tumbled into the camp of Midian; it came to a tent and struck it so that it fell and overturned, and the tent collapsed."

14. Then his companion answered and said, "This is nothing else but the sword of Gideon the son of Joash, a man of Israel! Into his hand God has delivered Midian and the whole camp." 15. And so it was, when Gideon heard the telling of the dream and its interpretation, that he worshiped. He returned to the camp of Israel, and said, "Arise, for the LORD has delivered the camp of Midian into your hand."

Knowing the frailty of human nature, the Lord gave Gideon a further confirmation to strengthen his heart for the warfare ahead. The Spirit of God had already infiltrated the camp of the enemy and had begun to unsettle some of the soldiers on their watch. Gideon was given another sign of God's sovereignty when, at God's suggestion, he and his servant Purah went down into the valley to hear what was being said on the enemy's front line. Stealthily approaching the outer ring of defense of the camp of Midian, they heard a conversation that dispelled any remaining doubt. If Gideon had ever doubted his own hearing, he had Purah to confirm what had been said.

Prophetic Dreams

One of the guards near the edge of the camp of Midian began to tell his comrade about a dream he had experienced. He'd seen a loaf of barley bread tumble into the camp of the armies of Midian, hit a tent, and totally demolish it. His fellow soldier instinctively knew the interpretation, and told the guard that it could only be "the sword of Gideon the son of Joash, a man of Israel! Into his hand God has delivered Midian and the whole camp" (v. 14).

When Gideon heard that, he took a moment to worship the Lord. Rising up, he returned to his three hundred men and upon arrival, he proclaimed to them the same words that God had spoken to him earlier: "Arise, for the LORD has delivered the camp of Midian into your hand" (v. 15). God had spoken, and now Gideon had spoken. The sword of the Lord had now been unsheathed, for when both God and man speak in unison, the sword of the Spirit is brandished in the earth. When God commands a man to speak, even to a valley of dead, dry bones, if that man speaks with God's voice behind him, the bones will live! (See Ezekiel 37.)

This "partnership in voice" is not just desirable, *it is essential.* God is a speaking God, and because He continues to honor the authority of man, which was given to Adam in the Garden, He will always look for a man to stand in agreement with Him and pray: "Your will be done, on earth as it is in Heaven." As the psalmist said, "The heaven, even the heavens, are the LORD's; but the earth He has given to the children of men" (Ps. 115:16). Every time the Word of God is spoken through the mouth of man, that Word becomes prophetic in nature, by the very fact that the breath of God is in it. Not only can the inspired Word be used to comfort, encourage, and edify the people of God, but it can also carry revelation as it did in this case with Gideon.

The early church of the New Testament derived great benefit from prophetic speaking and revelatory experiences. When the apostle Paul went to Jerusalem to see the apostles and elders, he went under the revelation and guidance of the Spirit. The church at Antioch was able to prepare for world events after the prophetic words of Agabus, who predicted by the Spirit that a great dearth was soon to come. This actually took place in the days of Claudius Caesar. The same prophet at a later date was also able to warn Paul of events that would take place in his personal life if he chose to go to Jerusalem.

The Scriptures are full of examples of prophetic dreams and utterances where the Lord has communicated His will. Indeed, when Jesus was a child, his life was spared when God spoke to his father Joseph in a dream and caused him to take the holy infant out of danger.

Prophetic Revelation

The prophetic word is a conduit of the voice of God to us. Dangers of incorrect interpretation that have accompanied this kind of ministry have caused many to omit it altogether! While this is understandable in many cases, it is unfortunate that many churches have slipped into a position where they secretly—or openly—despise prophesying.

People who have done this certainly don't want to hinder God and quench His Spirit. But the damage that has affected people through impure prophecy has caused them to avoid the field of revelation completely. It is sadly true that sympathy for this position is sometimes warranted. Nevertheless, the Scriptures abound, both in the Old and New Testaments, with examples of revelatory, prophetic messages. If saints in the past have greatly benefited from this kind of ministry, then we should, too!

For the man who is walking in the Spirit, the past revelation of the Scriptures and the present illumination of the Spirit are his life! He needs a God who has spoken and settled His Word forever, and he needs the same God to speak to him in the very present. This is the balance that keeps him in position and in relationship with the Almighty.

For the man who is not walking with the Lord, even though he might profess a Christian faith, prophetic revelation isn't required. For the most part, this man is following his own plans. He doesn't need *"ears to hear"* because a deep inner life is not a priority to him.

However, the man who walks *with* God is kept in a continual state of trust and needs the Lord to speak to him regularly. Prophetic words and dreams become intensely important to keep him in the perfect will of God for his life. If God was ever to call you into missions, you will find that the revelation of the Spirit is indispensable, because it can open the heart of an individual or a community to the Gospel message. When a man of God reveals something by the Spirit that he could not have possibly known, it convinces the hearers of the validity of the ministry, and they will say, "God is in him, of a truth!"

As a missionary to Russia for many years, I have had the gracious experience of receiving revelation for the people I ministered to. On my first visit to that country, I visited a large city, which had through the Soviet years, been a *"closed city"* due to the military installations existing there. Even the Russian people had difficulty visiting the area. My visit took place during the early days of the collapse of the Soviet Empire, and fear, suspicion, and lawlessness were in the air.

My host was an English teacher at the local university. One evening she brought her best friend to share an evening meal with us. Her friend spoke English very well, as her job was in Russian stocks and shares. We had very pleasant conversation throughout the whole evening. We retired to bed that evening, but I couldn't sleep. I kept thinking about my host's friend, and my spirit was troubled over her.

Instinctively, I felt that she had skipped over some vital things in her life. I sat up in bed and began to pray, upon which I saw in my heart and mind, a revelation of her husband. All she had told me the previous night was that she no longer had a husband. In the revelation, I saw him tormented in flames and full of anguish over his wife and child, regretting bitterly the fact that he was not with them and that he had done something wrong against them. He was desperately seeking his wife's forgiveness. With this picture came a word that would only mean something to myself or somebody from my locality where I lived in the north of England. The word was *Scarborough Bridge*!

As that word came, I saw another picture that showed him falling from a great height. I knew instinctively that this man had committed suicide by throwing himself off a high ledge, for the bridge in northern England had been notorious for suicides until the local police made changes to make it impossible to access. After breakfast the following morning, I talked with my host and shared the things the Lord had shown me.

She nearly fell over! "How did you know?" she asked me. Apparently, this man had been involved with a nefarious crowd. He owed them a lot of money and feared for his life. In a moment of desperate panic, he had thrown himself off a high-rise block of apartments. I asked my host to share all the revelation with her friend at a time when she felt it would be right.

When I returned to that city a year or so later, I was a little reluctant to meet this man's wife again, not knowing what effect my words might have had on her. I need not to have worried. With face aglow, she flung her arms around me and thanked me for being obedient to the "heavenly vision." Neither she nor I fully understood all the reasons for this disclosure, but she told me that upon hearing the message through my host, she had sunk into a deep depression for four days.

On the morning of the fifth day, she woke up feeling completely different. It was beyond her full understanding, but she just felt totally released from the pain of her grief. For the first time since her husband's death, she and her daughter were looking forward to a more hopeful future.

Looking at her bright face that day, I didn't doubt it! Clearly, a deep work of forgiveness had taken place in her heart. I just quietly thanked God for His individual care for this woman.

Not only do we need prophetic revelation to release individuals, but we also require it for our own guidance and protection. Too many times, zealous Christians have gone into a foreign environment with an attitude of "Let's kick the Devil out of here!" They have presumed that because they are positioned as "seated" with Christ's authority, they can launch an attack any time they want and expect the powers of darkness just to run out of town! They have adopted a cavalier approach to ministry, thinking that the strong man will allow the spoiling of his goods without a fight.

They fail to realize that most of the time, the "rulers of the darkness of this world" have the permission of God to be where they are! Unless God decides to take issue over their territorial possession, the man of God will do well to consult the Lord first as to what action is to be taken. Sometimes, the Lord will allow things to continue as they are. He knows best, and we do well to remember that all the thrones and dominions of darkness in opposition to Him are still serving Him! (See – Colossians 1:16). The battle belongs to the Lord, and we are His servants.

The armies of Midian were to be destroyed by Gideon because their time was up. The Lord had decreed judgment against them. All spiritual battles against the enemies of God begin in heaven, and then play out on earth. Any attack against Midian before this would have resulted in defeat for Israel, because heaven had decided that Midian would rule Israel for seven years. Likewise, the defense of Jerusalem in A.D.70 was futile, because heaven's counsels had determined desolations upon the city. Similarly, it was going to be like this for the host of Midian, for no matter how many warriors they brought to destroy the land, desolations had been determined upon *them* from the throne of God. The outcome was always going to be total defeat.

Wisdom and knowledge teach the man of God when to go out to war and when to stay at home. Wisdom and knowledge teach him how to understand the times and if it is a time for war, then these two revelatory gifts will help him understand the strategies of God for the hour.

Seeking God for this ministry of prophetic revelation is of paramount importance. Many have marched straight into enemy territory with loud acclamations of the Lord's approval upon their endeavors only to find that the enemy has laughed at their efforts. Clearly, they did not have the Lord's approval! The only approval that they had was their own. They ran into the enemies' camp with only the *"sword of Gideon!"*

The enemy only fears when the *"sword of the Lord"* is against them. Who is Gideon, and what is his sword, if the Lord's sword is not involved? Who is Moses, and what is his staff, if the rod of God is not involved? Who is David, and what is his sling, if the name of the Lord is not involved?

There was a missionary from Texas who led a mission team to a notable, ancient city in Europe. This man had a "hang 'em high, wanted dead or alive" approach to the powers of darkness over that city. He had the whole team primed to "take the city for Jesus" and "kick the devil out of town." Off they went, but within two weeks, the team was back home, and he was undergoing treatment for depression. Clearly this man possessed zeal, but was lacking in wisdom and understanding. His prideful attitude had blinded him to the true situation, and the enemy struck back.

Sometimes men of God forget that the main focus of ministry is leading souls to Jesus through the message of His cross. The apostle Paul had personal treasuries of prophetic revelation, but he kept himself on course with his message of "Christ crucified." If the holds of evil spirits *have* to be broken, then let the man of God walk in step with the Spirit so that there is authority in his words. Let him seek the Lord for wisdom and understanding to protect himself and effectively deliver others.

Prophetic revelation is *so* helpful for front-line pastors and missionaries on the field of God's work. Not only is it helpful, it is *so* comforting to know that God is truly with them and assisting them in all that they do. This was Gideon's experience that night, for the revelation given to him that evening not only strengthened him to make war, it also comforted his soul, knowing that God had done this just for him.

In the sphere of revelations from God, it's interesting to note that the sword of Gideon was pictured as a loaf of bread. A loaf of bread does not immediately speak of a weapon of warfare, but herein lies a secret to the wisdom of God. Who would have thought that a rod could exhibit so much power in the land of Egypt? Who would have thought that the jawbone of an ass could inflict such a defeat upon the Philistines? Obviously, that which seems of little consequence to men can prove to be the cutting edge for God. A tumbling loaf of bread that carries heaven's approval can become a weapon of mass destruction against the enemy.

Oh that we would give ourselves to know His ways. Even if what He calls us to do seems a puzzle to our understanding, let us defer judgment upon the matter until later, for the wisdom of God is rarely appreciated in the immediate. However, eventually, "Wisdom is justified by her children" (Matt. 11:35).

On a personal note, having been involved in the humanitarian side of the Gospel in some poor countries of the world, the freely given bread to the hungry has turned out to be a wonderful sword of the Spirit to bring them to Christ. Bringing the love of God through medical and social care has initiated breakthroughs in some communities for the Gospel message, proving time and time again that it's much easier to preach to the "five thousand" after you've fed them!

CHAPTER TEN
A TIME OF WAR

The waiting was over. Preparations had been done. The time of war was upon Gideon and his three hundred men. The purposes of God had brought a new season in the life of Israel. It was "a time to kill" (Eccles 3:3).

JUDGES 7:16-25

16. Then he divided the three hundred men into three companies, and he put a trumpet into every man's hand, with empty pitchers, and torches inside the pitchers. 17. And he said to them, " Look at me and do likewise; watch, and when I come to the edge of the camp you shall do as I do: 18. " When I blow the trumpet, I and all who are with me, then you also blow the trumpets on every side of the whole camp, and say, 'The sword of the LORD and of Gideon!'" 19. So Gideon and the hundred men who were with him came to the outpost of the camp at the beginning of the middle watch, just as they had posted the watch;

111

and they blew the trumpets and broke the pitchers that were in their hands. 20. Then the three companies blew the trumpets and broke the pitchers—they held the torches in their left hands and the trumpets in their right hands for blowing—and they cried, " The sword of the LORD and of Gideon!" 21. And every man stood in his place all around the camp; and the whole army ran and cried out and fled. 22. When the three hundred blew the trumpets, the LORD set every man's sword against his companion throughout the whole camp; and the army fled to Beth Acacia, toward Zererah, as far as the border of Abel Meholah, by Tabbath. 23. And the men of Israel gathered together from Naphtali, Asher, and all Manasseh, and pursued the Midianites. 24. Then Gideon sent messengers throughout all the mountains of Ephraim, saying, " Come down against the Midianites, and seize from them the watering places as far as Beth Barah and the Jordan." Then all the men of Ephraim gathered together and seized the watering places as far as Beth Barah and the Jordan. 25. And they captured two princes of the Midianites, Oreb and Zeeb. They killed Oreb at the rock of Oreb, and Zeeb they killed at the winepress of Zeeb. They pursued Midian and brought the heads of Oreb and Zeeb to Gideon on the other side of the Jordan.

Since the battle for Jericho in Joshua's day, there had never been such a seemingly foolish plan of attack, but Gideon was determined to obey the Word of God whatever the outcome. Quickly, he divided the three hundred into three groups. He put a trumpet into the hand of every man and gave each one an empty earthenware jar that concealed a flickering flame inside. With final instructions commanding them to imitate everything he would do, they all made their way down to the outer ring of the enemy's defense. Arriving at an opportune time, after the middle watch of the night had just taken up their positions, Gideon seized the moment. Before the watch could settle into their work of vigilance, their sleepy eyes were startled by the shrill sound of trumpets and the breaking into flames of torches all around them!

Added to all that was the surround sound noise of an ambush on the greatest of scales as the men of Israel lifted up their voices saying, "The sword of the Lord and of Gideon!" Every man of Israel stood in his position, blowing the trumpet, waving the torch, and exclaiming with a loud voice, "The sword of the Lord and of Gideon!"

Panic seized the sleepy hosts of Midian and in the confusion of the night, they began to fight amongst themselves! Confederacies always run the risk of disintegration, and certainly a nation that had two kings like Midian would have invariably had the seeds of bipartisanship. But whatever the thoughts that gripped their frightened hearts that night, it all resulted in them killing each other, at least for the initial stages of the battle.

The Momentum of Victory

The remaining host of Midian began to flee out of the valley and head for home, but the remaining men of Israel who lived in the areas of Naphtali, Asher, and

Manasseh gathered themselves together and pursued the Midianites. Realizing that many of the enemy would seek to return homeward via the flat Jordan valley, Gideon sent messengers throughout all the mountain area of Ephraim, asking them to come down and take the waters of Jordan to cut off their escape.

The men of Ephraim responded and took all the waters of Jordan as far south as Beth Barah. In the ensuing slaughter, they found two princes of Midian among the foe. The two princes were called Oreb and Zeeb, and they were famous in Midian. They both perished that day at the hands of the men of Ephraim. Oreb the *raven* and Zeeb the *wolf* were slain at two different places, but their decapitated heads were brought to one place in the end, which was at the feet of Gideon. (In the intense heat of battle, every warrior knows who the real leader is.)

What a day of victory it had been! What an unforgettable morning in Israel! Once again, the day had proven: *"The foolishness of God is wiser than men, and the weakness of God is stronger than men"* (1 Cor.1:25). Once again, the weak things had confounded the things that are mighty. The man that the Lord had first found hiding by the winepress in fear of the Midianites was now standing at the head of the armies of Israel with the first trophies of war at his feet! Truly the Lord was right—this man was a mighty man of valor - even when God *first* spoke to him. Gideon couldn't see it at the time, but now his courage was apparent to everyone—including himself!

Lessons in War

The sword had been in his mouth! The *shout of a king* had been in his voice, and together with three hundred men the Lord had totally vanquished the enemy. So it is with us who are armed with the fire of God's Spirit in the "earthen vessels" of our lives. With the testimony of Jesus on our lips, God causes us to triumph in every situation we encounter. Walking with God in this world will eventually lead us into times of conflict with the enemy but from the experience of Gideon, we can learn some vital keys to victory. Apart from all the principles learned from Gideon before the conflict, there are moments in the battle itself that can also teach us vital lessons.

Obeying orders

One of the first lessons we can learn is the obedience exhibited by the three hundred men of Israel toward the commands of Gideon. Unity behind the vision of God's chosen man is powerful on the field of battle. Not only were they unified in the cause behind their courageous leader, they proved to be men of true valor themselves! They were commanded to imitate Gideon and to remain in position until God had broken through.

In today's world of independent attitudes, this *"remaining in position"* has become an alien concept to many. Only a few will put their trust in the leader and commit themselves to the vision he is carrying. Understandable as this is in light of the many indiscretions and sins of present-day leadership, the problem of trust still remains. For many, the issue of trust has completely broken down.

Nevertheless, if anything is going to be accomplished for the kingdom in our times, then trust must be restored. These three hundred men trusted Gideon with their lives, and as a consequence of that, they all held their positions in the valley. Truly, the leader who can garner that kind of loving commitment will be able to attempt great things for God. Even in the face of failure, he will still command the respect of his people, for although no one following him wants to be unsuccessful, most good people can handle honest failure. What they cannot handle is the greed and lust of self-promotion.

Optimum moments

In every conflict, there are optimum moments for decisive action. Throughout history, generals on the field of battle have known this to be true. When Gideon and his men approached the outer ring of defense, they timed their attack to perfection. While the new watch was just getting into position and sleepy eyes were just readjusting, Gideon seized that moment to blow the shrill sounds of three hundred and one trumpets and to surround the camp with three hundred and one bright flames. He and his men also shouted the prophetic word of God, declaring, "The Sword of the Lord and of Gideon!"

It was the moment. If a man of God in leadership should possess any spiritual gift, it should be the ability to recognize the optimum moment. Not only does he need to know that moment...he must also be able to restrain his followers until that time, because if he listens to his people's assessment of the situation, he will probably act sooner than he should.

Napoleon Bonaparte, the famous French leader in the battlefields of Europe, knew this lesson of the optimum moment. Positioned upon the high hills of the battlefield, observing the conflict with his generals, he would wait for the optimum moment. Many French troops would be engaging the enemy, and often the battle would go back and forth all day. Waiting in the background was the famous Old Guard. These were his special troops, and they had a proven record of invincibility. There were reasons for that. One of the reasons was that they were only employed in the field when the optimum moment had arrived. On many occasions Napoleon's generals would gather around him insisting that the optimum moment to introduce the Guard had already arrived. "Sire," they would implore, "surely the moment is now!"

But Napoleon would respond, "Wait, wait."

"But Sire, we protest," they would argue. "We must send in the Guard now!"

"I said wait!" Often the actual optimum moment came well after the younger generals had made their assessments, but the experience of Napoleon taught him otherwise. When Napoleon perceived the moment, the Old Guard was sent in, and the invincibility they had enjoyed continued for many years, largely because their leader knew the optimum moment and had the ability to "seize the day."

So it is with any leader involved in God's work. He must learn to recognize the optimum moment and gently but firmly resist the clamor of inexperienced voices around him who would put pressure on him to react too soon.

The hour and the man

History is grateful for the courage of the three hundred men of Israel, but *one* man secured the victory. "Thou shalt smite the Midianites as one man!" The Lord spoke those words to *Gideon* to assure him that the battle would be more a case of "one on one" rather than "one against the many." When the message of the prophetic dream describing the loaf of bread smiting and demolishing the tent of Midian had been determined as Gideon's sword, it was settled in heaven that this hour was to be largely met by one man.

When in any age, an hour of crisis comes upon the scene of time, though many will respond to the call, there always seems to be one man who rises up in the crisis and makes the grade. To such an individual as this, the current crisis is never a total surprise, for in his heart there is a feeling that he had been prepared for that very hour. A sense of destiny now steels his nerves, and when given an opportunity to lead, he takes up his position to serve.

Winston Churchill, the great Prime Minister of Britain during the Second World War, confessed his sense of destiny, remarking that his whole life up to that point had been a preparation for that dreadful hour. So it is within the life of the Church in every generation in both universal and local settings. In every congregation experiencing great blessings from God, in the midst of it all you will find a man who has been singularly favored by the Lord to command the work. Sometimes that *singularly favored one* might not even be there, but may have passed on into the next life! But because promises were made to him in his days on earth, blessings are now raining down on the work of his hands.

This was the situation in the kingdom of Judah when, after the failings of Solomon and his children, the throne was kept in blessing for a long time to come because of the promises made to David when he was alive. Great men like David, though taken from the scene of time, have a lasting effect, and their works are not forgotten but indeed follow them into succeeding generations.

"I sought for a man among them" are always the words of a searching God, whose eyes are continuously scouring the earth for a man with whom He can show Himself strong.

The crisis

Victory of any consequence will always require crisis and risk. In a world full of the selfishness of men, God, in His eternal purposes, will call for a crisis in order to change things. As He called for famines in the days of Joseph and Elisha, so the Lord will work in all generations to create desperate times to fulfill His will. But before those times come upon a people, He has already made provision by preparing individuals for leadership through those times. In this we see the goodness and the severity of God. A careful study of Bible characters will reveal that men of valor have been prepared to step into the crisis long before it actually took place.

Why a crisis? The answers are not always plain, but we do know that it sometimes takes large events to change history. Events of this magnitude are dark moments in human history, but the repositioning that has ensued has very often been for long-term benefit. The challenge for the man of God is to step into the crisis and confront the issues head on.

This is the hour that only the truly courageous take on, because they know that they will be judged by the outcome. It will require them to *"lay it all down"* and expose themselves to the risk of failure. But if the Lord is with them, the hour of crisis will identify them in victory forever! We all know about Daniel and his friends because their hour of crisis identified them forever in their victory over flames and the jaws of terror! So it is with any man of valor, in that the crisis will lift him from the ordinary to the extraordinary if he rises to the occasion.

What was it that made Moses a great man? Was it not the crisis in Egypt? What was it that made young David a great soldier? Was it not the crisis with Goliath? And what was it that made the Lord Jesus such a great Savior? Was it not the crisis of lost humanity? Let us not fear the crisis, but let every man of God seek the Lord for what his role might be in it! The present challenges can be your greatest gift!

Joshua and Caleb did not fear the challenge of taking possession of the land God had promised to His people. They urged immediate conquest of the land, knowing that God was with them and that even the giants were "bread" for them. When God allows a giant to emerge out of the background, you don't have to fear the fact that he is ranting and raving and causing all kinds of distress. In actual fact, he is being fattened for the slaughter. As the saying goes, "The taller they are, the harder they fall."

The head of Goliath belonged to young David on that day of confrontation, and the host of Israel knew it. The heads of Oreb and Zeeb belonged to Gideon on his own victory day, and all the men of Ephraim knew it. And the head of the serpent belonged under the foot of Jesus on the day He was resurrected, and all the foes in hell knew it! To the victors belong the spoils!

Sour Grapes

In a large family, there always seems to be a whiner amongst them. There's usually one who will feel he is "called" to complain. Jealousy of others is at the heart of it all and it manifests itself in continual faultfinding and antagonism, especially of the openly successful.

Ephraim and his descendants seem to have inherited this attitude, for on more than one occasion, the men of Ephraim begrudged the personal victory of someone else. This was true in our story of Gideon.

121

JUDGES 8:1-3

1. Now the men of Ephraim said to him, "Why have you done this to us by not calling us when you went to fight with the Midianites?" And they reprimanded him sharply. 2. So he said to them, "What have I done now in comparison with you? Is not the gleaning of the grapes of Ephraim better than the vintage of Abiezer? 3. God has delivered into your hands the princes of Midian, Oreb and Zeeb. And what was I able to do in comparison with you?" Then their anger toward him subsided when he said that.

It was to be an attitude that the Ephraimites would pay for dearly in the days of Jephthah, a later judge of Israel. Their knee-jerk reaction of crest-fallen pride kicked back at Gideon for his wonderful success, but Gideon calmed their angry jealousy with a denigration of himself and his people compared to the illustrious reputation of the Ephraimites. He did what not many men can do—he took a "back seat" for God. He was determined to get the job done. That is a characteristic missing in many leaders today. Gideon cared little for momentary praise. He was glad to share it, as long as the work went on and the task got finished.

It appears that for every man of God who is openly successful for the kingdom, along the way he has to contend with the accusations of his brethren. People who should know better find it hard to admit that without a man like Gideon in their lives, they would still be languishing in mediocrity. It's hard for a man to feel the need for another. Furthermore, in a democratic world of equality, it is difficult to embrace the thought that somebody else is over you, even in the Lord.

Nations that have a background of monarchy have a better understanding of the government of God and can submit more readily to a leader set by God through theocratic means. While the "many" are content to feed on the average, they secretly know that they need the charismatic individual, who with God-given flair and ability, can arrive on the scene and minister with aplomb. With great relief they welcome him, but after a while the applause of inaugural days recede, and undertones of complaint eventually begin to surface. Lack of appreciation kills the spirit of a charismatic leader because he knows in his heart that without his abilities, the very ones who chide him would be totally lost without him! It's very hard for a highly gifted man to bear these inconsistencies.

There's nothing so difficult to handle as war within "the house." Sometimes, the turmoil is completely the leader's fault, and he stands culpable before God and the people for his errors. Sometimes, and this is the hardest of all, the Spirit of God has directed him in a way that has brought genuine upset to many in the congregation. At these times, people have seemingly justifiable grounds for complaint, especially when they feel that they can't understand what is taking place, and their very understanding of Scripture is being tested!

There is trauma that is felt by both sides in a situation where everyone wants God's best but the leadership is compelled to follow the Holy Spirit's guidance in a way that proves unusual or just different. When no one is doing anything wrong, and yet there is disagreement in the camp, only a spirit of loving grace will heal the rift. This situation is indeed a crisis. But it may be a crisis initiated by the Spirit of God! He looks beyond the present to see the needs of the future, and change, however uncomfortable today, must take place for the "wineskin" of tomorrow.

Lonely Path

Times of disruption, especially those times when jealousy has been the root of resistance, can be the most lonely of moments to walk through. The man of God will have to call on all his patience to continue dealing in gentleness and stop him physically leaving town! This was the path of the Master. He was tempted to leave the mission of the cross altogether. But he refused the voice of the enemy and committed himself to the task by setting his face toward Jerusalem. He was to die for the world, but he would be *"wounded in the house of His friends."*

The lamentable thing about these kinds of wounds is that they seem to draw more blood than others. With deep sadness, the apostle Paul wrote to Timothy reminding him of what he already knew—all the brothers in Asia had turned away from him. (See 2 Timothy 4.) Paul expressed to Timothy the confidence that although Demas and all but Luke had left him, he knew that God would never leave him: "But the Lord stood with me and strengthened me" (2 Tim. 4:17).

This is what the man of God should always remember. No matter what happens, no matter where the conflict comes from, the Lord will always stand by you! When the arrows of rejection have sunk their points deep into your heart, remember the words of Jesus who said, "Father, forgive them, for they do not know what they do" (Luke 23:34). Walk on. Walk on in peace and *"let His gentleness make you great!"* (Psalm 18:35).

Great men are known by their beneficence as well as their accomplishments.

"I Alone Am Left"

The words of reply from Elijah to the God of earthquake, wind, and fire in 1 Kings 19:14 resonate deeply within the hearts of all true men of valor. The grandiose decisions Elijah made on Mount Carmel brought deliverance to Israel, but isolation to himself. Fleeing the raging retribution of the authorities of the day, he ran to the southernmost border town in Israel, and for further good measure, he traveled into the wilderness another day's journey!

The right decision will not always be welcome! Most men of God understand that fact of life, but many men are still surprised when the right decision has not been warmly received. This can happen even in a marriage. A husband's resolve is put to the test when a decision he has made has not been warmly accepted by his spouse. "Can two walk together, unless they are agreed?" is a wonderful maxim of truth (Amos 3:3). It can be readily said that if God is going to call the one, He will call the other too. But while that is true in the general call of God, there does come times in the heat of battle when decisions about life and ministry must be made— decisions that may not meet with instant agreement. In war, decisions must be made. Sometimes they are right. Sometimes they are wrong. Nobody is perfect!

Ideally, a man and wife in ministry together should always see eye to eye on everything, but that's not true to life's experience. Every man of God should know that there are times in life's battles when decisions have to be made that will cause severe stress between him and his wife. The natural dissimilarities between the sexes manifest themselves in different thought processes that can cause a rift in the relationship.

There will be times when your spouse will think that you are "just plain wrong." The atmosphere within your home may be fraught with tension over a decision you made that is questionable, and your judgment can been scrutinized. There seems to be no winners at this point. Even if you are right, your joy at making a correct decision will be accepted—but rarely applauded. If you are wrong in your discernment, you will have to accept all the responsibility for its damaging outcome.

No wonder James admonished us: "Not many of you should presume to be teachers, my brothers, because you know that we who teach will be judged more strictly. We all stumble in many ways" (James 3:1–2). The task of leadership is immense, but someone has to do it! Man must take the lead and do his best, even if he finds himself walking a lonely path and finding himself exiled in the "wilderness" for a bad decision. In such moments, he will do well to remember that the LORD has not abandoned him and furthermore, He has already made arrangements for his recovery!

What is the alternative? Make no decisions? How do you change the world with no decisions? One can ask any soldier of any era who has survived the traumas of total war if all the decisions made during conflict were good ones. Invariably, he will tell you story after story of brilliant conquest and ironic tragedy that ensued from military decisions. There are no fatalities that carry such sadness as those who lost their lives to *"friendly fire."*

When David was fleeing for his life from the hand of King Saul, his decision to visit the Levitical city of Nob had tragic consequences. (See 1 Samuel 21.) Ordinarily he would not have been in such a frightening situation, but war is war, and he was treading a lonely path—a path that caused him to make decisions that would cost others dearly. Young David received the refreshment he needed at Nob, but a spy in the city saw him and told King Saul where he was. As a result, all but one inhabitant of that city perished by the brutality of Doeg, the Edomite. (See 1 Samuel 22:6–23.) When news came to David, he took the pains of responsibility by telling the sole survivor that he had caused the death of all that man's family. (v. 22.) From that day, David took Abiathar, that young man, and made him as one of his own men.

The man of God must be willing to walk the path of temporary isolation and to endure the standoffishness of all around him as he makes what he thinks are his best decisions in the circumstances. He must also be willing to seek forgiveness and reparation if damage has ensued. Some mistakes can be compensated for, and some can't be rectified at any price. Not every decision will be a good one, but some one has to give the orders. Someone has to take charge; it may as well be you!

CHAPTER ELEVEN
TAKING CARE OF BUSINESS

I t's never over *'til it's over!* There's no substitute for complete and total victory. The temptation to settle for less than complete victory comes when the day has been won and the enemy is limping home. To leave the task unfinished is to invite trouble later, because the enemy that can limp all the way home, can regroup to fight another day! There's a big difference between a wounded enemy and a dead one.

Young David killed Goliath of Gath, but the giant had brothers who later returned to torment Israel. So it is with us, that one major victory doesn't guarantee us peaceful tomorrows unless that victory was total and complete. We too must finish the job and take care of business. When God gives the promise of victory, all his enemies are to be scattered! All the arrows of the Lord's deliverance must be spent against the enemy. It was revealed in later years by Elisha the prophet to the king of Israel that the king through *prophetic deed* must smite the ground many times to signal the total annihilation of the enemy. (See 2 Kings 13:14–19.) Let us all learn this lesson well. It will please the Lord and save us many unnecessary hardships ahead.

Gideon instinctively knew that although the "day" had been won and the heads of two Midianite princes were in his possession, there was still business to attend to. Victory would not be complete until the kings of Midian were either captured or killed.

Having had no sleep, and having literally fought the "good fight of faith," Gideon and his three hundred weary men began the chase for the kings (Judges. 8:4).

JUDGES 8: 4-12

4. When Gideon came to the Jordan, he and the three hundred men who were with him crossed over, exhausted but still in pursuit. 5. Then he said to the men of Succoth, "Please give loaves of bread to the people who follow me, for they are exhausted, and I am pursuing Zebah and Zalmunna, kings of Midian." 6. And the leaders of Succoth said, "Are the hands of Zebah and Zalmunna now in your hand, that we should give bread to your army?" 7. So Gideon said, " For this cause, when the LORD has delivered Zebah and Zalmunna into my hand, then I will tear your flesh with the thorns of the wilderness and with briers!" 8. Then he went up from there to Penuel and spoke in the same way. And the men of Penuel answered him as the men of Succoth had answered. 9. So he also spoke to the men of Penuel, saying, "When I come back in peace, I will tear down this tower!" 10. Now Zebah and Zalmunna were at Karkor, and their armies with them, about fifteen thousand, all who were left of all the army of the people of the East; for one hundred and twenty thousand men who drew the sword had fallen. 11. Then Gideon went up by the road of those who dwell in tents on the east of Nobah and Jogbehah; and he attacked the army while the camp felt secure. 12. When Zebah and Zalmunna fled, he pursued them; and he took the two kings of Midian, Zebah and Zalmunna, and routed the whole army.

Pursuing the Kings

Crossing over the border, Gideon and his men came into Gilead, where the tribes of Reuben, Gad, and half of Manasseh had taken possession of the land on that particular side of the Jordan River. Many years beforehand, Moses had established their inheritance, but when he first heard of their request, he was very angry with them. Moses scolded them for their unwillingness to go over into the "promised land" and reminded them of what had happened to the congregation of Israel after their first refusal many years prior. However, they calmed his spirit when they committed themselves to go over Jordan to fight the battles of the Lord and enable the other tribes to take their inheritance also. (See Numbers 32.) They agreed to fight until the land of Canaan was conquered, and then they would return to Gilead where their families had been living in safety. The fear of God's judgment to make *another* generation wander in the wilderness concluded their deliberations on this matter. They did the right thing in the end but their selfish motives had been revealed. A legacy of "what's good for us?" seemed to permeate the ethics of later generations in Gilead as the *"me first"* attitude had continued to dominate their hearts and minds.

Gideon was about to meet this attitude in the immediate cities of the land. He would find, to his disappointment, that not all men had faith. People who are preoccupied with "what's good for them" will invariably be "strangers" to the good fight of faith, because they will risk nothing for the kingdom. These are symbolic of brothers in Christ who will build social and financial towers for themselves to help them feel secure. Though they *talk the talk*, their lives are always made bare when a true man of God arrives on the scene. A lifetime of self- indulgence is shamed by the lean, warrior-like features of a man whose life has been on the battlefields for the kingdom. The contrast between such men might not be readily seen, but close observation over time reveals where true stature exists.

We see this principle displayed in our story of Gideon:

5. Then he said to the men of Succoth, "Please give loaves of bread to the people who follow me, for they are exhausted, and I am pursuing Zebah and Zalmunna, kings of Midian." 6. And the leaders of Succoth said, "Are the hands of Zeba and Zalmunna now in your hand, that we should give bread to your army?"

—vv 5–6

Arriving at the first city on the other side of Jordan, Gideon asked the men of Succoth for some food for his troops. He told them his mission in pursuing the kings of Midian (for it was in their interests too), and waited for their reply. It seemed that the men of Succoth had *fully* adopted the *"me first"* approach to life and derided Gideon with cruel mockery. It was a common thing in the warfare of those times that body parts would be cut off the vanquished and laid in heaps, and so the men of Succoth asked Gideon if he already possessed the hands of the kings of Midian.

It's possible that the leaders of this city would have desired to give assistance to Gideon and his men, but they weren't prepared to run the risk and jeopardize their future livelihood. Alas, Gideon did not find men here like himself. They did not resemble the "children of a king," and true nobility was not to be found in Succoth. The calculated minds of political expediency would never allow their own resources to be given away, especially when there was a possibility of future retribution from the enemy. Faced with too much personal risk, the men of Succoth took the cheap way out and flatly refused to help their brothers. Gideon rebuked them for their selfishness and promised to return and punish them severely.

Only a true shepherd will put himself in "last position" for the benefit of others. He will lay down his life for God's sheep. As Gideon led his flock through Gilead, he would find a repeat scenario at the next city called Penuel.

Then he went up from there to Penuel and spoke to them in the same way. And the men of Penuel answered him as the men of Succoth had answered. So he also spoke to the men of Penuel, saying, "When I come back in peace, I will tear down this tower!"

—vv. 8–9

Words of judgment were spoken against both cities, and a promise was made to return and execute that judgment upon them. Little did these cities realize that the "sword of the Lord and of Gideon" was against them, and little did they realize that judgment was arriving the next day!

Finishing the Job

Another battle was about to take place, a battle that would have normally been ridiculous to initiate because of the overwhelming odds. But this battle was no problem for Gideon's army of three hundred men. Fifteen thousand enemy troops remained, but the "sword of the Lord and of Gideon" was against the kings of Midian, and a covering of invincibility had descended upon the men of Israel.

Gideon had quickly learned the principle that - it is inconsequential to the Lord to save the people of God by many or by few. Under the cover of evening darkness, Gideon and his men came upon the camp of Midian from a direction they didn't expect and at a time they weren't prepared for. Tightly gathered together, the host of Midian became a more manageable target, and

Gideon wrought havoc amongst them. The two kings, Zebah and Zalmunna, fled the scene, but were captured by the men of Israel.

10. Now Zebah and Zalmunna were at Karkor, and their armies with them, about fifteen thousand, all who were left of all the army of the people of the East; for one hundred and twenty thousand men who drew the sword had fallen. 11. Then Gideon went up by the road of those who dwell in tents on the east of Nobah and Jogbehah; and he attacked the army while the camp felt secure. 12. When Zebah and Zalmunna fled, he pursued them; and he took the two kings of Midian, Zebah and Zalmunna, and routed the whole army.

—vv. 10–12

Tired but exultant men began their journey home. Total victory had been accomplished. The Midianites had been destroyed, and their two kings were now their prisoners.

The Sword of Gideon

JUDGES 8:13-17

13. Then Gideon the son of Joash returned from battle, from the Ascent of Heres. 14. And he caught a young man of the men of Succoth and interrogated him; and he wrote down for him the leaders of Succoth and its elders, seventy-seven men. 15. Then he came to the men of Succoth and said, "Here are Zebah and Zalmunna, about whom you ridiculed me, saying, 'Are the hands of Zebah and Zalmunnah now in your hand, that we should give bread to your weary men?'" 16. And he took the elders of the city, and thorns of the wilderness and briers, and with them he taught the men of Succoth. 17. Then he tore down the tower of Penuel and killed the men of the city.

In the early hours of the morning, returning homeward, they found a young man from the city of Succoth. They asked him for information concerning the leaders of the city. It was determined that seventy-seven men constituted the eldership of the city. Gideon set off to punish them for their refusal of assistance the previous day. It seems to be one of life's ironies that they who adopt a *"me first"* attitude usually fall to someone else who exhibits the same selfish approach! Is it any surprise that the young man being interrogated should quickly save his "own skin" and betray the leaders of his city?

Finding that there was no spirit of self-sacrifice in the young man, Gideon got the information he was looking for. In fact, the young prisoner was willing to identify everyone! May this lesson grip the heart of every man who continually considers himself more highly than others for there will always come a day when loyalties will be sold and betrayals will abound. There's never any true love lost between selfish people.

Approaching the city, he quickly dominated the people and took the leaders by force. Putting them to open shame, he and his men punished them by whipping their bodies with thorns and briars taken from the wilderness. That same day he also visited the other city that had refused to give him help, and he broke down their tower of defense as he said he would. The bodies of the men of the city littered the streets as the sword of Gideon bathed itself in blood.

18. And he said to Zebah and Zalmunna, 'What kind of men were they whom you killed at Tabor?' So they answered, " As you are, so were they; each one resembled the son of a king." 19. Then he said, "They were my brothers, the sons of my mother. As the LORD lives, if you had let them live, I would not kill you." 20. And he said to Jether his firstborn, "Rise, kill them!" But the youth would not draw his sword; for he was afraid, because he was still a youth. 21. So Zebah and Zalmunnah said, ' rise yourself, and kill us; for as a man is, so is his strength." So Gideon arose and killed Zebah and Zalmunnah, and took the crescent ornaments that were on their camels' necks.

After the judgment of Succoth and Penuel, Gideon then began to pass judgment on Zebah and Zalmunna, the two captive kings of Midian. If there had been any chance of mercy for these two kings, it all evaporated when, upon enquiry, Gideon learned that they had killed some of his brethren at Tabor. Had these two kings shown mercy at Tabor, Gideon would have shown mercy to them that day. But because they had earlier wantonly killed the men of Israel, Gideon pronounced the death sentence upon them. Turning to his eldest son, Gideon commanded him to kill the two men. But being a youth, he feared to draw his sword and do the execution.

At this, the two kings asked Gideon to execute them, for, although they didn't want to die, if they must, it seemed better to them to be slain by another king. Gideon rose up, drew his sword, and slew both of them right there and then. Their dead bodies signaled the final word of complete victory.

The enemy had not just been subdued, but it had been *totally* annihilated. The carcasses of the kings of Midian lay motionless on the earth. Gideon and his men had taken care of business. Gideon also took away the rich ornaments that had been on the necks of the king's camels.

Scripture makes it very clear that God will not give His glory to another, nevertheless, there are times when He will give certain, yet restrictive, power to the men He uses. Elisha recognized this endowment of authority in the life of his master Elijah. When the time was approaching for Elijah to be taken up to heaven away from him, Elisha asked him for a double portion of his spirit. Elijah replied to Elisha that he had asked a difficult thing, but promised him that he would be granted his request if he saw Elijah's exit from earth (2 Kings 2:10). Elisha stuck with his master all the way to the end, and his desires were met when the mantle of spiritual power fell off Elijah and was left behind. God was present in all of that magnificent scene, but it was Elijah who granted the request!

After the Lord had opened the door of opportunity to Solomon to ask what he wanted from Him, he requested wisdom and knowledge. The Lord, who had made him king over His people, gave him those things and everything he could wish for. (See 1 Kings 3.) The God of Israel began pouring in the riches of His kingdom and put them at Solomon's disposal!

At the end of this present age, the Lord will raise up two witnesses who, through the prophetic nature of their ministry, will execute judgments in the earth according to their own will (Rev. 11:3). There will be restrictions upon their life span and upon their powers, but they will be able to smite the earth with plagues as often as they will!

It seems that when a man honors God's Word, then God honors that man's word. When, under the unction of the Holy Spirit, Gideon lifted up the sword of the Lord with voice and trumpet, God then lifted up the sword of Gideon! While license cannot be taken in these matters, there does appear to be a generous degree of latitude given to God's man of the hour. This was the kind of scope that the Lord gave to Saul through the prophet Samuel. The prophet anointed Saul to be king and predicted the signs that would take place to confirm his calling to be sovereign over the nation. He then told Saul that once these signs were fulfilled, he was to do whatever his heart wanted to do because God was with him! (1 Samuel 10:7).

How awesome is this bequeathing of God's own power! How amazing that the Lord of the universe would give such authority to men! And how glorious is man's future with God that Adam's race will enjoy dominion again with the Living Lord.

CHAPTER TWELVE
REIGN OVER US

F lushed with their remarkable success, the men of Israel approached Gideon and virtually offered him the crown. So great was the elation amongst them that they hurriedly gave a prospect of future dynasty to the house of Gideon, reaching to at least the third generation! The Midianites had been utterly defeated, but now the real enemy of Israel had arrived in a different form. The wicked kings of Midian were easily recognized as belligerent, but would Gideon recognize the "impostor" now knocking at his heart's door?

Would Gideon understand that a personal victory over possible disaster could be undermined by imprudent triumph? The war against the Midianites was over. But now the scene of battle changes, and the decisions made during the accolades of victory will shape the next generation in Israel. Winning the peace can be harder than winning the war! Gideon must be as careful now as when he first decided to fight the armies of Midian. Will personal triumph be his undoing?

22. Then the men of Israel said to Gideon, "Rule over us, both you and your son, and your grandson also; for you have delivered us from the hand of Midian."

—Judges 8:22

Purple Gown

In the earlier part of his experience, Gideon had taken upon himself the "scarlet robe" of suffering, and prepared himself to risk his life for the will of God. Whatever it took, Gideon was prepared to pay a personal price for victory. Obedience to God's will was always going to be expensive for him, but with great courage, he went into great areas of risk to fulfill the purposes of God.

From the robe of suffering, Gideon then put himself into a position to receive the "blue mantle" of the Holy Spirit's power. He had the wonderful thrill of being endued with *power from on high* as heaven came down and clothed Gideon with authority. He had become a holy vessel for God to use.

These principles of separation had been instituted many years previous through the ministry of Moses. (See Numbers 4 :4-15) A tabernacle of God's presence was built, and every time the tent had to be disassembled to allow the camp of Israel to move forward, Aaron the high priest, and his sons would wrap the Ark of the Covenant in the veil of the most holy place. Thereafter, they would proceed to wrap the holy vessels in cloths of blue. In the blue cloths, they would wrap the ark, the golden candlestick, the golden altar and the table of shewbread. Upon the utensils and the bread of the table of shewbread, they placed a cloth of scarlet, symbolic of the One who would come to give the bread of His own life for the children of Israel and the whole world. This "One" to come would give His own blood to cover the table of the Lord. The instruments then employed would not be spoons and dishes - they would be hammers and nails.

The remaining piece of holy furniture was the brass altar, and both it and all its utensils were wrapped in a cloth of purple. The ashes of the fire were taken away and a purple cloth was spread over it. Throughout history, purple fabrics belonged to the rich, the noble, and the royal. This royal color of imperial crimson casts its dye on the throne of God's altar, for it is here and only here, where kings are made! When the *finger of God* touches the heart of man, a new man is made in the earth! Spontaneous combustion burns up *the flesh* and a *new creature* walks out of the flames. It is here, in the burning fires on the altar, that heaven touches earth. The blue of the "spiritual" is infused with the red of the "natural."

In this baptism of fire, the "offering" becomes a royal gift ascending back to God. The Messiah to come would walk through these fires, crowned with thorns and covered in a purple robe. Such is the mystery of royalty with the Almighty God. Amid the greatest of fiery trials, true kings arise. In the fire upon the altar, God enters into the flames and clothes His servants with the purple gown of royalty. And only those who have been with God through the furnace can wear it!

Gideon has now walked through the fire, and royalty with God is now his possession. The people's desire to have a king to rule over them found its full expression when they came to Gideon and imploringly said these words. "Rule over us." What was Gideon going to do?

Getting it Right

But Gideon said to them, "I will not rule over you, nor shall my son rule over you; the LORD shall rule over you."

—verse 23

The noble Gideon made the best decision he knew how to make. Out of the integrity of his heart, he kindly declined the offer and reaffirmed the theocracy of God amongst them. *"The Lord shall rule over you,"* he said. Gideon refused the position of royalty. He did the admirable thing because most men, given the opportunity for personal advancement on that scale, would have probably grabbed it immediately.

For Gideon, the soldier in him was the driving force in his life. His commitment to *serve* God produced the *"Brave-heart"* character he had become. Seeking the throne had never been in his mind, and so with little difficulty, he firmly dismissed the offer. Having said that, every soldier wants an honor, a medal, or a reward.

The position of king had been quickly declined, but the trappings of royalty suddenly became very appealing.

Getting It Wrong

24. Then Gideon said to them, "I would like to make a request of you, that each of you would give me the earrings from his plunder." For they had golden earrings, because they were Ishmaelites. 25. So they answered, "We will gladly give them." And they spread out a garment, and each man threw into it the earrings from his plunder. 26. Now the weight of the gold earrings that he requested was one thousand seven hundred shekels of gold, besides the crescent ornaments, pendants, and purple robes which were on the kings of Midian, and besides the chains that were around their camels' necks.

—verses 24–26

All of a sudden, the benefits of successful leadership overtook Gideon. Knowing that he held the esteem of all the men of Israel, and knowing that they would deny him nothing, he requested the golden earrings that the men had taken from the dead bodies of the enemy. Earrings seemed a small request, but when all the treasures were gathered together, there was a great weight of gold. Each man gave his spoils and gladly threw his earrings into a large single garment, and Gideon walked away that day a very rich man.

It probably would have been better for Gideon and for Israel if he had accepted the leadership of the nation and left the money to others. By conquest, he won the right to rule and the people were willing to have him as their Judge. Gideon was set for a wonderful life in God, but *"sin was at the door,"* and he fell to it! He let down his guard and *sin crept into his house.* Oh that Gideon had passed this personal test! The Lord wanted him to rule. He just didn't want the gold to rule Gideon. This mighty man of valor was God's choice but indulgence would prove his undoing! How sad it is to realize that the true enemy of Israel had won back some of his ground on the very day of Israel's victory. Amid the hoop-la of public excitement, when the enemies of Israel seemed defeated forever, Satan was coming in through the back door totally unhindered!

Brother, is this ever a lesson for you and me, - that personal victory leaves us just as vulnerable to attack as an all out offensive against us! *"Watch and pray, lest you enter into temptation!"* were the words of Jesus. How many men throughout history have unwittingly set into motion their downfall by decisions made in their hour of triumph?

Truly, the poet Rudyard Kipling in his poem of how to be a man, warned us of back door temptations.

"If you can dream - and not make dreams your master; If you can think - and not make your thoughts your aim; If you can meet with Triumph and Disaster, And treat those two impostors just the same"......

We all fear disaster. But do we also fear triumph? Both have the potential to destroy us, so let us fear God, fear ourselves and humbly thank God for every victory He gives.

God will give you triumph because He wants to rule through you. The rule of God still comes through chosen vessels just as it has always done. The Lord raised judges up not only to deliver the nation from their enemies but to *rule* Israel and *prevent* apostasy happening again, at least while they were alive! Sadly, Gideon allowed triumph to become a problem to himself, his family, and eventually all of Israel. Winning the war would prove to be the easy part!

Getting It Wrong—Again

Returning home to Ophrah, no doubt to a hero's welcome, Gideon melted the gold he'd been given and then *made the biggest mistake of his life!*

Then Gideon made it into an ephod and set it up in his city, Ophrah. And all Israel played the harlot with it there. It became a snare to Gideon and to his house.

—verse 27

It's possible that the motivations of Gideon's heart may have been good when he made the golden ephod, but it was something he did that failed to have God's blessing upon it. When David was king in Jerusalem, he wanted to bring the ark of God into the city called by his name. Believing that God had also chosen Jerusalem, David quickly brought the ark out of the home it had been located in, only to walk into disaster. (See 2 Samuel 6.)

David meant well, but he didn't have God's blessing upon his actions. It wasn't until later when David decided to go very carefully with the Lord and resolved to do everything by the Book that success eventually came. David learned a serious lesson concerning the worship of the Living God—everything must be sanctioned first. God's things must be handled God's way.

Gideon's request for the gold might have had good intentions. He may have thought that a scriptural symbol might have adequately taken the place of idolatrous Baal worship in his own town. But one thing is for certain—he didn't have God's blessing to do it. Good things are not necessarily God's things. We do well to remember that it was the pursuit of the knowledge of good as well as evil that cost our first parents the Paradise of God. The man of valor must be aware of the good as well as the evil, for good things can still bring forth death, but God's things will always bring forth life!

The *ephod* was a priestly vestment that the Lord instituted through Moses. (See – Ex. 28) It was to be worn by the priest and fastened upon the two shoulders where the two stones of memorial were fitted, bearing the names of the children of Israel. This holy vestment was central to the whole regalia, because the golden breastplate of judgment was attached to it. The breastplate held the precious stones naming the twelve tribes of Israel, and the mysterious Urim and Thummin. These two mysterious stones along with the ephod and breastplate were the means whereby the children of Israel could enquire of the Lord and obtain answers. Everything God told Moses to make was uniquely set apart for service and like the anointing oil of priestly service, any copies were strictly forbidden.

All these things had been established in Israel, but idolatry and rebellion had dimmed the eyes of successive generations. Spiritual decline had robbed the children of Israel of true light and understanding. Gideon might have thought to himself that a golden ephod was not like the obviously idolatrous Asherah pole or the altar of Baal, but that God would be pleased with a *scriptural* symbol as an object of worship.

Alas, for Gideon, he was soon to learn that idolatry is idolatry, whatever the symbol! The Bible says, *"And all Israel played the harlot with it there"* (v. 27). The same spirit of immorality that had expressed itself in and around the Asherah pole was bringing its unclean spirit on the people again. Gideon should have known better! He should have realized that even a religious symbol without the sanctioning of God would bring a curse upon the people.

One of the signs of maturity in God is when God will not just discipline you when you are disobedient, but He will also discipline you when you have inadvertently done something wrong on the premise that you should have known better! Gideon should have known better, and there was trouble in his house after this whole episode.

As it was in Gideon's day, so it has been through the centuries. Former victories have corrupted their way when men have chosen to immortalize their memories.

Without doubt, religious spirits have shown some of the greatest opposition to the work of God. Empty symbolism has stolen the hearts of many, and although the symbols may have had a scriptural reference, the life of God has been absent. Icons can only *remind* us of God, but the Spirit can *refresh* us with the ever-present life of God! In the early 1900's, wonderful revival came to the valley communities of Wales and thousands were touched by the power of God. However, it became very difficult for successive generations to move forward with the Lord. So great was the outpouring in the early days of the last century, that even decades later there were visible symbols of God's power literally hanging on the church walls. Rows of crutches and other similar devices still hung on the back walls of many churches as a reminder of what God did. Unfortunately, those symbols of past victory had unwittingly undermined the ministries of future generations. True, they were great reminders of the past, but they hindered the ministry of the future because the concepts of what ministry is and how it should be done were frozen in time. It became almost impossible to lead many Welsh people into new *pastures* of ministry because the current ministry was always being measured by the past. To be fair to the people who came through the fires of revival, it was very difficult for them in the ensuing decades to see what was passing for "ministry" compared to what they had seen. They were like the old men in Ezra's day who though rejoicing in that they were seeing the work of God resume in Jerusalem, could only weep at the thought of how good things were before, when the first temple was standing in its glory. (See – Ezra 3:12)

The lesson is simply this; that we must worship God for who He is and not just for what He does! What God does is variable. Who God *is* remains rock solid. What God does can sadly be imitated and idolized. The wonderful trophies of a revival can become relics but when we worship God for who He is, we find stability in our lives and an openness to hear what He is currently saying.

Clearly, Gideon's golden ephod was unacceptable to God. Sadly, it affected everyone. It became a blot on the life of Gideon, and it ensnared his whole family. His mistake would cost him dearly. The altar of Baal was broken down, but probably on a rock nearby, a golden ephod had been lifted up in full view, and the "eyes of Heaven" were shedding tears again.

It seems from historical observation that the hardest places for God's "revival fire" to fall are on the "altars" where it had fallen previously. In such situations, the enshrinement of past victories can blind the people of God with pride and can only compel God to burst forth in other areas. The victory of one generation can be a hindrance to the next. This situation became apparent in Gideon's own town, for not only did the *local* people worship the ephod, the children of Israel came from *everywhere* to pay homage! Ophrah had unwittingly become a center for religious devotion and idolatrous worship, making its spiritual condition worse than before!

Upon his return to Ophrah, Gideon had also built his own home and had begun to make his own way in life.

28. Thus Midian was subdued before the children of Israel, so that they lifted their heads no more. And the country was quiet for forty years in the days of Gideon. 29. Then Jerubbaal the son of Joash went and dwelled in his own house. 30. Gideon had seventy sons who were his own offspring, for he had many wives. 31. And his concubine who was in Shechem also bore him a son, whose name he called Abimelech.

-- verses 28-31

If Gideon had shown restraint in refusing the crown, he did not curb himself with the pleasures of women, for he had many wives. We don't know how many children he had altogether, but we do know that he had seventy sons born to him. Not satisfied with the love of many wives, Gideon ventured "further a-field" and sought the physical pleasures of a slave girl. It was to be a relationship that would prove to be a curse on his family. Gideon was blessed with seventy sons, but a dark shadow of tragic destiny was cast over them when a son was born to Gideon through this woman. The idolatry of the golden ephod had opened up a spiritual door of evil, and through the birth of Abimelech, the cold hand of death had begun to take its icy grip upon the family. Nevertheless, while Gideon was alive, that generation of the children of Israel enjoyed peaceful quietness for forty years.

Courage to Fail

How tragic that a man like Gideon – a mighty man of valor, should have such a reckless attitude to the spiritual health of his family. His failures were completely his fault and while God was good to Gideon, keeping him in a life of peace, disaster waited to engulf his family after his passing away. Mistakes! Is it possible for you or I to get through Christian life without mistakes? You will find in your life, two kinds of mistakes being committed. There are honest mistakes and there are dishonest mistakes when selfishness has proven to be the ulterior motive. But mistakes made in sincerity have always been easy to forgive by both God and man.

A blacksmith in England said to his apprentice, on the day the young man started work. "Son, the man who hasn't made a mistake, hasn't made anything! But measure everything twice and cut only once!"

Never were truer words spoken, for indeed, the man of accomplishment will have done so imperfectly. The true condition of the human heart, coupled with the intensity of life's pressures, inevitably reveal the inadequacies of man. Errors of judgment will be made, and the man who doesn't want to make a mistake should stay curled up at home!

As the life of Gideon has already taught us, there is a war going on all the time, and the man who bravely enters this conflict will probably encounter the carnage resulting from bad decisions that he has made! Coming to terms with one's own failures and their sad results can be the most painful of exercises, because most good men want to accomplish things for God without a single mark against them! They honestly desire that they should get things right every time. But in the intensity of life's battles, their humanity doesn't score very high. For a man who likes to be in control and have all the relevant information at his fingertips, these moments become a living nightmare, because a perfect assessment of the situation is not always available.

Sometimes the man of God doesn't have the full picture, and his understanding may be limited. Yet the moment requires a decision. He is forced to decide upon a course of action that has a high risk factor and a strong possibility of failure. Moments like these reveal the presence of true valor, for when failure is possible, the man of God still marches forward advancing the kingdom and prayerfully leaving the outcome to God.

The question that must be asked is this; "Is failure final?" The intimidation of failure is the ominous sense of finality it produces in the human heart. The pain of *"appearing to be wrong"* is more than most can bear, and a man will do many things to preserve his blushing face. This has very serious consequences for the ministry, because the well-worn path of "safe success" is chosen over the unknown trail of the pioneer. Originality in the ministry becomes the first victim in a war that wants to neutralize the whole army of God. Like a row of Russian dolls that not only replicate each other, but also come out of each other, the cutting edge of God's Word is often blunted by empty sameness. When this kind of situation prevails, the best the people of God can do is maintain what has already been, because no new ground is being won.

Winning is great, but losing also has its merits. Most inventors have failed in their experiments many times over. But with each failure there has come the knowledge necessary for advancement. During World War I, surgery practice and procedures knew astonishing success as doctors and nurses fought to keep the wounded troops alive. Failures were many, but what could they do? They had to try unusual techniques and be original in their ideas, because they were facing wounds that they had never seen before. Advancement came to that branch of medicine because they had *"courage to fail."* It would have been easier for the surgeons to play it safe, but the lives of severely injured men were dependent on them.

So it is with men of God in today's world. Originality and risk are part of the territory. Courage in ministry is very expensive, demanding every ounce of personal commitment to willingly face the danger. But let every man of valor remember the words of a previous great leader of men, who said with conviction: *"Do not rebel against the LORD, nor fear the people of the land, for they are our bread; their protection has departed from them, and the LORD is with us."* (See- Num 14:9) The secret to successful ministry is to be God's man and be your self! Walk hand in hand with God. Give to the world that which God has uniquely given you. That is where you will find your "sword" – out of your personal experience with the Lord. Spiritual treasures will pour out of your life whenever you share your testimony to what the Lord has done. There's no short cut to spiritual wealth. Let every minister of God remember that cheap success for him means starvation for his congregation. Only those men who have been through the baptisms of their own fiery trials of faith can feed the flock of God and bring true wealth into their experience.

Such men have heeded the counsel of the Lord and have bought from Him "gold, tried in the fire," thus making themselves rich in faith. These are the gladiators in God's arena, and they *"bear not the sword in vain."* Holding to the conviction that it's better to have fought than not to have fought at all, such men of valor have their wounds of failure soothed in the ointment of forgiveness. They dust themselves down, get back in the saddle again and ride off into the future. They stand as pillars in the kingdom - as men who have something to say!

What do we do with our mistakes? First, remember that the Lord is always ready to forgive us. He not only paid for our sins, He also covered all our failures when He became the perfect sacrifice at Calvary's cross. Second, many who may have been hurt by our bad decisions have made some bad decisions themselves and are only too willing to forgive you of yours if you ask them. To those who will not countenance you and neither forgive nor forget, their sin remains, but you must commit everything to the Lord and go on. The job needs to get done!

The man of God who wants to do great things for God will most assuredly have some experiences of regret. But as the blacksmith said to his apprentice, "Measure everything twice!" If you measure everything twice you will increase your chances of cutting only once. Diligence will save the man of God from many errors as he measures his words and actions, but the arrogant leader will undoubtedly leave behind him a trail of bruised and hurting sheep.

Having accepted the inevitable weaknesses in human leadership, let us also remember the goal of completeness portrayed in the Scriptures by James, who added this admonishment to leadership; "If anyone does not stumble in word, he is a perfect man" (James 3:2).

The Party's Over—Again

32. Now Gideon the son of Joash died at a good old age, and was buried in the tomb of Joash his father, in Ophrah of the Abiezrites. 33. So it was, as soon as Gideon was dead, that the children of Israel again played the harlot with the Baals, and made Baal-Berith their god. 34. Thus the children of Israel did not remember the LORD their God, who had delivered them from the hands of all their enemies on every side; 35. nor did they show kindness to the house of Jerubbaal (Gideon) in accordance with the good he had done for Israel.

—Judges 8:32–35

Gideon had won peace with God both for himself and for his whole generation, but another generation had arisen. As it was in Egypt in the time of Israel's great deliverance, "Another king arose, which knew not Joseph" (Acts 7:18).

The peace bought in one generation may not last during the times of the next. Gideon died an old man and was buried at home in his own community, but as soon as he was dead, the restraints upon the children of Israel were once more cast off! Once again, without a man of God to judge them, the children of Israel sank into depravity. Immorality abounded. To add further insult to the God who had saved them, they made Baal-Berith their god! *Baal-Berith* means "lord of the covenant," and they willingly sold themselves to this false god and ensnared themselves with covenants, pacts, and agreements with gods and men.

This web of dark deceit hurled the nation into the abyss once again, and the scene was set for them to devour one another in murderous ways. Not only had the children of Israel forgotten the Lord that had so wonderfully delivered them, they also chose to disrespect the sons of Gideon. They willingly forgot all the kindness that their father Gideon had done for Israel. The cycle of sin had returned, but a whole generation had known peace in their times, because of the Sword of the Lord and of Gideon.

CHAPTER THIRTEEN
TRANSFORMING POWER

There are many principles to learn through the life of Gideon, but from the many, two essential elements emerge to take preeminence. These two fundamental truths of God were in operation before the life of Gideon, and they remain in operation even unto this present day. They are the principles of redemption, which reveal the power of God to release a soul from slavery through a ransom and to convert that soul into a new man for eternal glory.

Blood Offering and Faith

From the time our first parents received a *covering* for their nakedness and the sacrificial offering of lambs was given by *faith* through their son Abel, the principles of redemption have clearly appeared time and time again. These two principles became the currency of God's kingdom in which those things lost in darkness could be redeemed and brought back to the Light of Himself.

This economy of blood offering and faith encompassed the whole ministry of Moses. The people of God were delivered from slavery in Egypt by the blood of a lamb and by the people's faith in God. All these early types and shadows met their final destination in Jesus of Nazareth, who, being the very Son of God, paid the price of release for all mankind. It was He who gave His own life upon a cruel Roman cross. By so doing, He gave the world its greatest blood offering.

When faith is added to Calvary's offering, the blood of Jesus becomes immediately efficacious, and the soul that believes will be converted into a new man. The redemption process rests on these two pillars of truth. It is through *"faith in His blood"* that the transforming power of the Spirit of God can act upon a man's life. Anything else is unacceptable, like the offering of Abel's brother Cain, who's offering of personal works, was refused by God.

Gideon experienced both these principles. Once his offering of a young goat had been accepted through the fire of God, he then believed God's Word and acted in faith. The blood offering gave him a *place* in God, and faith gave him *accomplishment* in God. Gideon's faith and courage were to become famous in the life and times of the nation. Even in the New Testament era, Gideon's feats were still well known. His unusual daring has been remembered and preserved forever, and his valor put him into the "Hall of Fame" in the kingdom of God (Heb. 11:32).

Transforming Words

It's a well-known fact that words have influential power. Like a sword in action, words can pierce the heart and strike a person with such force that it can be difficult to retain composure. It is no coincidence that in the House of Commons in the British Parliament, two sword lengths measure the distance between the two sides of the house. The war of words must know measured restraint, to avoid the blood baths of character assassination for political gain. On the other hand, softly spoken words, especially those blended with music can calm the most agitated of spirit.

Many words are said over our lives, and they can exercise their authority for positive or negative influence. But the words spoken by God will always be for our eternal good. When the Lord speaks a word over our lives, as He did over Gideon, we must believe it and act according to it—no matter what our circumstances are.

To Gideon, the man who was frightened of the enemy and spent most of his timid life in hiding, God came one day and said, "The Lord is with you, mighty man of valor!" Little did he realize that those words would change his destiny, and not only his, but the destiny of the entire nation! Those words caught Gideon by surprise, for he was exhibiting anything but valor whilst hiding by the winepress. But when the Lord had spoken, things changed.

Not only did things change for the better, they were transformed for God's glory! This word from God hung over Gideon's head like a ripened fruit. It was God's promise of victory. The time of harvest had arrived. By faith, Gideon picked the fruit of this promise and by believing the Lord's opinion instead of the prevailing circumstances, he rose up to be the man God had called him to be. By receiving this word of power, Gideon found himself consumed by the Spirit of God. The Lord clothed Himself upon Gideon and transformed him to become the captain of the victorious armies of Israel.

Transforming Presence

If a man like Gideon can have his life transformed – then so can you! However, the problem for many men today is not a lack of *receiving* God's transforming word, but *maintaining* God's word over a lifetime. Why are so many pastors leaving their posts? What ingredients are missing to cause their personal transformations to be only a temporal experience?

The answer to this growing problem of maintaining our Christian journey through life lies in two areas. The solution is found in *"position"* and *"prayer."* Too many have "bought into" a religion of feelings and experiences because that is what is sadly being offered in churches throughout the Western world. Today, what passes for Christian ministry is very often religious seduction for general appeal. In both pulpit and pew, this can only produce a fair-weather approach to wholly following Jesus. Doctrine becomes the first casualty as anecdote and personal testimony claim the pulpit time. Many don't live by the unchanging positional truths of the Gospel because they prefer to live by the feelings of the moment. While all experiences in God are valid, unfortunately they are not sufficient to maintain a whole life of service. No personal baptism of spiritual power is designed to last a lifetime! The apostle Peter received a wonderful baptism of power on the Day of Pentecost, but he had to be severely corrected by Paul some years later for a glaring error! (See - Gal 2:11) Peter's fear of others that had so dominated his life before his baptism of power surfaced again! Is it any wonder that the Scriptures encourage us to be continually filled with the Spirit? (Eph 5:18).

Without a clear knowledge of your unchanging position with God, you will lose your anchor in the storms of life. You don't have to *feel* a truth to experience its authority. You can *live* by a truth because it's an established fact! Truth is truth. Facts are facts. So then, live by doctrinal truth and let your feelings and experiences become subservient to your *"position."*

Added to your knowledge of position should be the abiding Presence of God through *"prayer."* So many men do not pray. So many ministers make no time to pray! How can you maintain your ministry if you do not pray? The veil of the temple was torn apart so that you could enter the most holy place of union with God. This is your position! Don't neglect the time spent in His Presence, because if you do, you will find it increasingly difficult to follow the path the Lord has chosen for you. At any time, you could be in danger of having your "house" blown down by the storm.

(See-Matt 7:25.) While you have been busy in other people's eyes, heaven has been watching you build your life on the "sand."

Jesus himself spent time with God. It was his pleasure and his comfort. Strength and direction were given to him in such moments. It was the nearest he got to heaven in his life on earth. It is not a coincidence that the Lord himself was transformed on the Mount of Transfiguration with heavenly glory when he prayed! (Luke 9:29).

Man of God, if you neglect His transforming Presence through *"position"* and *"prayer,"* you run the risk of failure. Don't let busyness ruin your ministry. If you totally engage your energies into activity alone, you will probably have a full calendar on your desk on the day you resign! Be observant in these personal areas. Keep in His transforming Presence. Change your *office* into more of a *study* and like the first apostles, give yourself to "prayer and the ministry of the word." (Acts 6:2)

Every Man

This divine process that Gideon passed through is the same for every man who desires to be used by the Lord. God has already made everything possible to fulfill your dreams. The initiative was taken a long time ago when His own Son gave Himself to the suffering of the cross, only to arise as the "Captain of our Salvation" and "Sovereign Lord" forever. Jesus of Nazareth will forever be God's "mighty man of valor."

Throughout eternity, everyone in heavenly glory will honor Jesus for his work as well as for who He is. The Lord Jesus went to war for us and endured all the crushing blows of sin upon his manly frame (Heb 10:10). The strength of his body was weakened in the conflict of the ages, but while he had a healthy body, he accomplished the will of God in His life with vitality. You will do well to remember that all your days are numbered just like his were! "Life" as you know it, will not go on forever. You must do what you can while you can.

Solomon, the Preacher, warned us all in his wisdom, that old age will come and take away the vigor of youthful powers, describing the gradual deterioration of our bodies in metaphoric language. Solomon described the legs of a man as "the men of valor," because it is the legs that empower a man for physical combat, and it's the legs that shake and knock together when fear has gripped the heart. (Eccles 12:3...Tanakh) So serve the purposes of God while you have the strength to do so and allow God to deliberately weaken you from time to time in order to make you spiritually strong! Like the apostle Paul, you will find that His grace is sufficient to get you through (2 Cor 12:9).

The patriarch Jacob was disabled by God in his thigh, in the very muscle of a man's strength, but rose up and found his destiny as a "prince with God and with men" (Gen 32:28). So it was with Jesus, that after his manly strength had been broken by God's will, he rose up and found his destiny as King of kings and Lord of lords! Upon the thigh of Jesus, God's resurrected Servant is now written this wonderful acclamation! Heaven proclaims again that this wonderful Man is the Word of God, the Father's Mighty Man of Valor, and the One who has brought many sons into heavenly glory. He did it all for us so that we can overcome in our lives and inherit the Throne of God. The ground has been won. The blood offering has been accepted. All that remains is for us to hear God speaking to us. All that matters now is God's opinion. All that's required is faith in action!

Gideon's life and the lessons within it are not just for existing leaders of the church today. They are for every man who loves the Lord. Any man who will open his heart to receive a word from God can be transformed by that word. The opinion of God is the edict of heaven. It is in fact a decree from the eternal throne! The exciting thing is this - that the Lord can come up to any willing man at any time and proclaim over his life, "The Lord is with you, mighty man of valor!"

Be ready! Wherever you are, be ready! Whatever you do, be ready! Behind the pulpit, behind the desk, or behind the wheel, be ready! In the factory, in the yard, or in the store, be ready! On the land, on the sea or in the air, be ready! Be ready for the Lord, for very soon, this temporal life will be left behind, and all its present trappings will become a forgotten memory. This scene of time will vanish forever, and you will soon find yourself before the throne, before the Lamb, and before your God! Be ready!

Do what you have to do! "The Lord is with you, mighty man of valor!"

Study Guide – For Group Discussion

<hr>

CHAPTER ONE

THE EYES OF HEAVEN

1. Read and discuss ISAIAH 59 – How far will God allow a nation to willingly forget justice, righteousness, truth and equity before His judgment comes?
2. How important is the local church in any society? What happens to the national church of any country when it no longer serves as "salt and light"?
3. How important are prayers of intercession to the health of a nation?
4. Discuss how God made the "wrath of men praise Him" in the life of Joseph.
5. What makes an empire blind to the "winds of political change"?
6. Discuss the power of the natural eye in a man's life – how is it a spiritual hindrance?
7. Share with the group how God has revealed new seasons of life to you.

CHAPTER TWO

THE VOICE OF THE PROPHET

1. Why does God often allow a national crisis to take place before He acts?
2. What do you think is the difference between "praying generally" to God and praying to God whilst under a "spirit of prayer"?
3. Are there prophets in the church today? Do we need prophets now?
4. Do we need to have God reveal things to us today – when we already have the Bible?
5. Does the Holy Spirit still send men to some places and forbid them going to others?
6. How important is the art of "listening" for men? Are you good at it?
7. Share a time when you heard God speak to your heart.

CHAPTER THREE

I SOUGHT FOR A MAN AMONG THEM

1. How important are the "hidden years" of preparation? Discuss the private years of the life of Jesus of Nazareth.
2. Discuss the relevance of "getting things right in the home" before handling things in the church.
3. Discuss the differences between a "calling" and a "sending" – e.g. Saul & Barnabas. How is a private preparation time of "calling" a future preservation from outside control at the time of "sending"?
4. Why do we need to know the "terror of the Lord" and the "love of the Lord"?
5. How does this balance of "fear" and "love" help us in our lives?
6. Discuss the importance of "going" when the "door" opens. Have you ever missed the optimum moment? Share with the group a time when you seized the opportunity at the right moment.
7. Discuss the dynamics of faith. How important is the "point of commitment" to the vision?

CHAPTER FOUR

CONFIRMING THE CALL

1. Why is it important that children receive the Lord into their lives? What advantages are there in early conversions with respect to future ministry?
2. Why does God establish His word through two or three witnesses? Why not one? What safety precautions are inbuilt for us in this matter?
3. Why is "timing" so important for us? What happens when we're early? What happens when our decisions have come too late?
4. Discuss the life of Joseph – in respect to the timing of God. Why do you think that the apostle Paul put patience at the top of his ministry list?
5. What are the advantages of waiting for the perfect timing of God?
6. What does Ephesians 2:10 mean – "doing the works He *prepared* for us to do"?
7. Discuss the importance of "sowing" into the next generation. Share a way you have already done this.

CHAPTER FIVE

KEEPING THE COVENANT

1. Discuss the topic of Bible covenants. Why did a covenant have to be "cut"?
2. How important to God is innocent blood? Are there severe penalties for shedding innocent blood?
3. How was Christ's sacrifice a fulfillment of all previous blood offerings in Israel?
4. Why is it important for men to intercede and "stand in the gap" for others? Why are prayer meetings generally attended more by women than men?
5. Why does the prayer of a righteous man "avail much" with God?
6. Discuss the spiritual bondages associated with broken promises, covenants, agreements, alliances etc.
7. Discuss the spiritual bondages associated with curses. Are curses real? Can curses exist where there isn't a cause for them? Can curses be broken? How important is repentance and forgiveness in these matters?

CHAPTER SIX

BREAKING THE CHAINS

1. Does fatherly headship transfer blessings? Can it transfer curses?
2. Is there such a thing as ancestral bondages? If so, can ancestral bondages affect a Christian?
3. Meditate on the lives of your own parents. What can you embrace from their lives and what should you avoid?
4. Did any of the spiritual problems residing in your parents already exist in the lives of *their* parents?
5. Why is it that family and cultural bondages are the most difficult to break?
6. Why are these kind of bondages so hard to recognize? Why is it important to break them *before* you begin public ministry?
7. What's in a name? Do personal names still carry any influence today?

CHAPTER SEVEN

CROSSING THE LINE

1. Why does God allow the enemy to go *just* beyond his boundaries?
2. Discuss the topic of "making bricks without straw." Why did God allow Pharaoh to make things worse for the children of Israel?
3. Why does God often allow us to be bruised or offended first? What advantages did Samson obtain from this principle?
4. Share an incident when you obtained the "moral high ground" and explain what advantage it gave you.
5. Why is personal weakness so powerful with God? How good are you at waiting?
6. How does "one man with God" constitute a "majority"? Read 2 Kings 6:8-23
7. The "limelight" of ministry – name three advantages and three disadvantages. Discuss the blessings of being in the ministry for a marriage. Discuss the pressures that ministry puts upon a marriage.

CHAPTER EIGHT

THE ECONOMY OF GOD

1. Why are the economics of God sometimes foolish to us?
2. Discuss the Biblical principles of "giving away" to receive back in abundance.
3. Discuss the prospect of walking through the misunderstanding of others, and looking foolish because of your obedience to God's ways. How would you handle things?
4. Do you know any pastor that has experienced a "Gideon revival"? How can you encourage such a man? Have you been that pastor? If so, how did you get through it?
5. Share a time when you have experienced the truth of "the Lord giving and the Lord taking away."
6. How important is the role of forgiveness in the life of a minister?
7. Why is maintaining the balance between the Spirit and the Word so important? What happens in a local church when there is too much emphasis on the Spirit. What happens in a local church when there is an overbearing emphasis on the Word?

CHAPTER NINE

STRENGTHENED BY THE PROPHETIC

1. Why is it important in ministry that God's word must become man's word? Why must the word become part of a man before he can speak it?
2. Does God need the voice of man at all? Why does He look for a man? Why does He reveal His secrets to His ministers? Read Amos 3:7
3. Is the gift of prophecy just for comfort, edification and exhortation? Can the gift of prophecy carry revelation?
4. Can prophets tell the future? Is this kind of foretelling ministry for the church today?
5. Discuss the *benefits* of prophetic ministry in a local church. Discuss the *dangers* of prophetic ministry within a local church.
6. How do "principalities and powers" though alienated in their hearts toward God, still serve Him? Read Colossians 1:16
7. Share with the group a moment when you have experienced a personal prophecy or a dream that had prophetic guidance in it.

CHAPTER TEN

A TIME OF WAR

1. Is war *ever* right for the Christian?
2. Strategies - does God need them? Do we need them?
3. How important is unity in a time of conflict? What happens to a nation when unity has been lost? What happens in a local church when trust has broken down?
4. Why do men continually misjudge other men? Why are they surprised when the "dark horse" wins? Why are men usually the "last to know"?
5. Crisis – friend or foe? Discuss the need for a crisis to be a catalyst for major changes.
6. Share a moment in life when a personal crisis became the "door" to another level of living – spiritual or natural.
7. Personal outward success – discuss the topic of petty jealousy in others. Who exhibits jealousy towards you – family, friends or strangers? How should a man conduct himself through it all.

CHAPTER ELEVEN

TAKING CARE OF BUSINESS

1. What has been a "Goliath" in your life? Is it dead? Has "Goliath" been a person in your life? Have you overcome them or do they still dominate your fears?
2. Goliath had four brothers – have you overcome those other problems in your life that were related to your "Goliath"?
3. Do you believe in symbolic power? Has God ever led you to do a prophetic deed?
4. Discuss the political expediency of the leaders of Succoth and Penuel versus the risk taking, doing what's right approach displayed by Gideon.
5. Have you ever acted with expediency and secretly failed to stand up and be counted over an issue? Have you ever "blown the whistle" on unrighteousness and paid a personal price for doing so?
6. Discuss the topic of Elijah granting Elisha's request for a double portion of his spirit. Read 2 Kings 2:9-15 Talk about the latitude of power that God gives His ministers from time to time.
7. How important is it to finish the job! Have you ever been *tempted* to settle for second best? Have you ever *settled* for second best?

CHAPTER TWELVE

REIGN OVER US

1. Discuss the inherent dangers of success. Why are rash words often said in the moment of victory? Have you ever made hasty promises in such moments?
2. What kind of man *wants* to be a king? What kind of man *doesn't* want to be king —yet *desires* all its benefits? What kind of man *doesn't* want to be king – and *desires none* of its benefits?
3. Why does God put his men through the fire? Why does he test men?
4. Gideon knew personal victory and personal defeat in the same day – has that ever happened to you? Have you ever "won in the morning" and "lost in the evening"?
5. Is it right for God to discipline His servant for an honest mistake? Should God ever use the rod of correction on His servant on the premise that His servant should have known better? Read 2 Samuel 6:1-9
6. Share with the group an honest mistake you made.
7. Discuss the spiritual problems of past revival victories in the minds of succeeding generations. Can something come from heaven in one generation and bring automatic life to the next? How long can "manna" from heaven last? Is church revival designed to go on and on, or is it for a designated time?

CHAPTER THIRTEEN

TRANSFORMING POWER

1. Is the spirit of the Age more male or female? Why do soap operas and commercials continually portray men as silly or "last to know" husbands? Why are kids portrayed as being smarter than their dads? Why are Ministers of the Cloth portrayed as old, charming, yet irrelevant men?

2. Why is the *voice* of a man preaching the word of the Lord so powerful? In charismatically gifted churches, why is it usually the women who speak in tongues or prophesy? Why are men largely absent from the local church prayer meeting?

3. Why are evil spirits sometimes pacified by worshipful music, yet become agitated when a man's voice rings out from the pulpit?

4. Do men need to cultivate their romantic side of their relationship with Jesus? Is it possible to go too far in this matter?

5. Why are men in church becoming more aware of their feelings? Is it a work of the Spirit? Is it the spirit of the Age? Is it a product of both?

6. Why is doctrine hard to digest for most people today? Why are personal testimonies and anecdotes so much a part of today's pulpit messages? Why do people want shepherds who are all "staff" and no "rod"?

7. Discuss the problems that face a fellowship when there is *no* judgment from the leadership. Discuss the

problems that face a fellowship when there is *only* judgment from the leadership.

8. Ask yourself one more question – "Can God choose me?"

Printed in the United States
50940LVS00005B/151-264